Mark Twain's Nevada

Samuel Clemens in the Silver State

Stephen H. Provost

Dragon Crown Books 2022
Fresno, California   ✦   Carson City, Nevada
San Luis Obispo, California   ✦   Martinsville, Virginia
All rights reserved

ISBN-13: 978-1-949971-32-3

Contents

Acknowledgements.

Thanks to Joe Curtis for an informative interview and the use of the photos in his collection. Deepest appreciation to Sharon Stora for her assistance in researching this project.

Maps.

Timeline.

1861

August 14— Arrival in Carson City

September — Expedition to Lake Tahoe, attempt to stake claim for timber cutting

December — Trip to Unionville, Humboldt County

1862

February — First letters to *Territorial Enterprise*, signed "Josh"

April — Arrival in Aurora

July — Aurora mayor gives speech at Independence Day gathering; copy of humorous address sent to *Enterprise*

August — Departure from Aurora

September — Paid $25 a week as city editor for the *Enterprise*

October 1 — First piece, "A Gale," published in the *Enterprise*

October 4 — "Petrified Man" hoax article published

December — Assigned to cover Territorial Legislature, courts in Carson City

1863

February 3 — First use of pen name "Mark Twain," in letter to *Enterprise* from Carson City

May — Two-month trip to San Francisco with Clement T. "The Unreliable" Rice

August 23 — Article on Steamboat Springs

September 8 — One-month trip to San Francisco

October — First Territorial Constitutional Convention begins in Carson City; Twain provides coverage for the *Enterprise*
October 28 — Empire City massacre hoax published
December —Artemus Ward in Virginia City

1864

January 29 — Death of niece, Jennie
May 17 — Article on Carson City fancy dress ball published
May 29 — Departure for San Francisco following resignation from *Territorial Enterprise*

1866

October 31 — Lecture at Maguire's Opera House, Virginia City
November 3 — Lecture in Carson City
November 7 — Lecture in Washoe City
November 8 — Lecture in Dayton
November 9 — Lecture in Silver City
November 10 — Lecture in Gold Hill, robbery prank

1868

April 23 — Hanging of John Millian, convicted of killing famed prostitute Julia Bulette, in Virginia City
April 27-28 — Lecture at Piper's Opera House, Virginia City
April 29 — Lecture in Carson City
April 30 — Lecture at school benefit in Carson City

1872

Roughing It published

MARK TWAIN'S

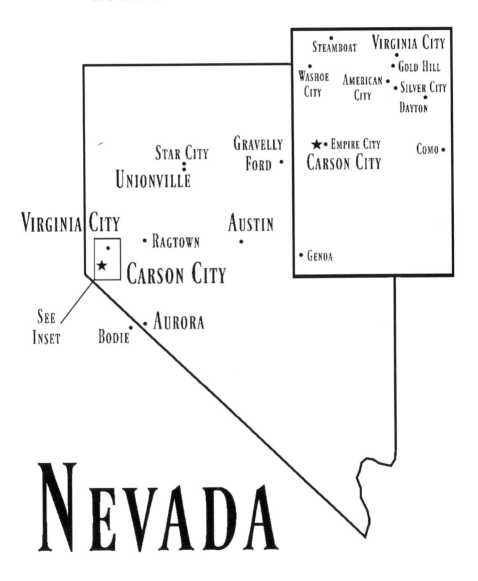

STEAMBOAT

VIRGINIA CITY

• GOLD HILL

WASHOE CITY

AMERICAN CITY

• SILVER CITY

DAYTON

★• EMPIRE CITY

COMO •

CARSON CITY

• GENOA

STAR CITY

UNIONVILLE

GRAVELLY FORD •

VIRGINIA CITY

• RAGTOWN

AUSTIN

★ CARSON CITY

SEE INSET

BODIE

• AURORA

NEVADA

STEPHEN H. PROVOST

Twain, center, flanked by George Alfred Townsend, left, and Buffalo newspaper editor David Gray. *Library of Congress*

Prefatory.

Why the word "prefatory" rather than "introduction"? For one thing, people tend to skip past introductions, and for another, it's the word Mark Twain used to introduce *Roughing It*, his 1872 work on his recollections of Nevada.

It's easy to read about a historical figure and imagining them walking the streets of the cities and towns where they lived as we know them today. It's natural to picture George Washington sitting in the Oval Office, even though the White House wasn't completed until the fall of 1800 — more than three years after Washington left office.

The same sort of impulse is present when we think of Mark Twain in Nevada. But Twain's Nevada was very different from the Silver State as we know it today. There weren't any bright lights. (There wasn't any electricity, for that matter). There were no casinos. There was no Las Vegas Strip. There wasn't even a Las Vegas: The city wasn't founded until 1905.

Young Sam Clemens.

There weren't really any cities, as we think of them, in 1860, a year before Twain arrived in Carson City — which itself was just a couple of years old. It was still part of the Utah Territory then, but it was already thriving: Its population of 714 that made it among the largest settlements in the region.

But by far the biggest community was Virginia City, where more than 2,300 would-be miners and opportunists had flocked with the discovery of gold and silver. Adjacent Gold Hill had a population of 638, followed closely by Silver City right next door at 637.

Nevada wasn't a state when Twain arrived, and Twain himself wasn't Twain: He still went by his birth name, Samuel Clemens.

That's how different things were.

Journalism was different, too. Twain didn't start out as a writer producing novels, but newspaper stories. He'd done some writing previously for his brother Orion's newspapers in Hannibal, Missouri, and Muscatine, Iowa, but he came into his own working as a reporter for the *Territorial Enterprise* in Virginia City.

Still, he wasn't your typical journalist.

Twain's approach can be summed up in his quote: "First get your facts straight. Then distort them at your leisure."

And distort him he did.

Sometimes, he even made them up out of whole cloth.

Reading through some of his newspaper accounts, it can be difficult to tell what's real and what's fanciful, but it's easy to see how he made such a name for himself writing fiction: He'd been doing it for years. As the pre-eminent practitioner of "sagebrush journalism," he relied on wit, satire, and outright hoaxes to entertain and inform his readers, peppering his news reports liberally with his own opinion.

Facts and opinions weren't attributed, as they would be today. They were merely stated, and this wasn't Twain's idea; When he was filling in as city editor, his boss, Joe Goodman, left him with explicit instructions not to pull any punches.

"Never say, 'We learn' so-and-so, or 'It is reported,' or 'It is rumored,' or 'We understand' so-and-so, but go to headquarters and get the absolute facts, and then speak out and say 'It is so-and-so,'" Goodman told him. "Otherwise, people will not put confidence in your news. Unassailable certainly is the thing that gives a newspaper the firmest and most valuable reputation."

Twain always seemed certain of his facts, even if they were fabricated in the depths of his fertile imagination.

"To find a petrified man, or break a stranger's leg, or cave an imaginary mine, or discover some dead Indians in a Gold Hill tunnel, or massacre a family at Dutch Nick's, were feats and calamities that we never hesitated about devising when the public needed matters of thrilling interest for breakfast," he admitted. "The seemingly tranquil *Enterprise* office was a ghastly factory of slaughter, mutilation and general destruction in those days."

Twain's style can make it difficult to tell what was real and what was fancy. Even in his own day, readers were sometimes confused — and outraged — when they discovered that Twain had told them a fish story. Other newspapers were chagrined to discover they'd reprinted what they thought were sensational reports sure to grab a reader's attention, only to discover there wasn't a lick of truth to them.

Twain was so controversial that the editor of a rival newspaper even challenged him to a duel.

They fought duels back then, even though it was supposed to be against the law. This was, after all, still the Wild West.

It wasn't the Nevada we know today. It was Mark Twain's Nevada, and that's the Nevada we'll be exploring in the pages ahead, where we'll follow in the legendary author's footsteps, visiting the places he lived and wrote about during his adventures and misadventures in the Silver State.

Most people know Samuel Clemens as a Missouri riverboat pilot, dispenser of quick-witted remarks, or the author of such classics as *The Adventures of Tom Sawyer* and *A Connecticut Yankee in King Arthur's Court*. He lived in Nevada for less than three years, but it was during his stay in the Territory that he adopted the name by which he would become known — Mark Twain — and met the man (Artemus Ward) who would give him the break he needed to sell his first successful story.

Clemens' time in Nevada was packed with adventures. He failed twice at prospecting for gold; set a wildfire at Lake Tahoe while trying to set up a timber operation there; worked as a journalist for the *Enterprise*; and witnessed the transformation of Virginia City from a mining camp into a true metropolis at the economic and political center of Nevada.

In Nevada, Clemens hobnobbed with the governor and cared for his sick brother. He worked for not one but two U.S. senators from the state. He formed a fast friendship with the man who became known as the first-ever standup comedian, the greatest humorist of his time (Ward, whose works Abe Lincoln reportedly quoted to open meetings of his cabinet.) One of his prospecting buddies (William "Billy" Clagett) was a lawyer who later served in Congress and introduced legislation to make Yellowstone a national park.

The editor of the *Virginia Union*, the *Enterprise*'s chief rival in Virginia City during Twain's tenure there, went on to serve as the defense lawyer for Brigham Young in a polygamy trial and got the Earp brothers and Doc Holliday acquitted after the gunfight at OK Corral. Twain may have even known Nevada's most famous prostitute, Julia Bulette, and he certainly knew her paramour, saloonkeeper, firefighter, and tough guy Tom Peasley.

At Peasley's saloon, he drank with a firefighter from San Francisco who claimed to have served as an inspiration for one of his most famous works.

Nevada shaped Mark Twain's life as much, if not more, than anything else. And this is how it happened...

Notes: In general, the subject is referred to as Samuel or Sam Clemens for events prior to his first use of the name "Mark Twain" in February 1863, and as Twain for events that took place after that. Pullouts titled **Getting to...** and **Key Sites** are designed to help the reader find key locations in Clemens' life.

American City.

American City, in an area known as American Flat, was one of four towns in the Virginia City area — the others being the main city itself, Gold Hill, and Silver City — and the only one not still in existence today.

The site, a couple of miles northwest of Silver City, was laid out in 1864 and boasted big ambitions: It wanted to be the capital of Nevada. At the time, that honor belonged to Carson City, but far more people lived in Virginia City and its environs, which served as the hub of Nevada business. So there was an argument to be made for moving the capital.

Founded: **1864**
Location: **Storey County**
Status: **No longer exists**

"We predict," the *Gold Hill Daily News* declared in January of 1864, "that in five years from now American City will be as large as Virginia [City] is at this time."

If the logic of this argument wasn't enough, the company that laid out American City offered to donate $50,000 to Nevada's coffers if the capital were moved. In addition, it promised to provide what the *Gold Hill Daily News* called "a splendid park containing 20 acres of land, besides several blocks of building lots." It was a not-so-subtle "incentive" — or bribe.

Another argument posited that Ormsby County, home to Carson City, had originally offered to furnish assembly rooms to the legislature free of charge. That offer had helped secure the state capital for Carson by a single vote. But once the prize had been won, the city had reneged on its offer and demanded a rental fee of $4,500 per session.

AMERICAN CITY HOTEL,

Near Rigby & Co.'s Quartz Mill.

WILLIAM FAWCETT, (Late of Sacramento) **PROPRIETOR.**

☞Table is furnished with all the delicacies of the season.☜
☞ BAR IS SUPPLIED WITH THE BEST OF LIQUORS.☜

Large and extensive Stables are connected with this Hotel for the accommodation of teams, etc.

BARTON LEE. J. T. KEEPERS.

WILLOWS SALOON,

AMERICAN CITY.

A place of Resort, Amusement and Refreshment. A Race Track always ready.

BARTON LEE & J. T. KEEPERS, PROPRIETORS.

Ads for American City businesses as they appeared in the 1864 city directory.

In light of all this, the *Daily News* correspondent in Carson was sure that the American City bill — introduced in the Assembly by Sam Clemens' friend and former prospecting partner William H. Clagett on February 15, 1864 — would pass both houses of the territorial legislature. It would then become law "unless the governor should veto it (we certainly expect better things from the old Governor)."

The following day, Mark Twain wrote a piece on "The Removal of the Capital" for the *Territorial Enterprise*, throwing his support behind the proposal. His main argument was that the press would be better equipped to keep an eye on lawmakers if they were to meet in Virginia City.

"While it remains in Carson," he wrote, "the Legislative Assembly is beyond the pale of newspaper criticism." It was therefore "beyond its restraining influence, and consequently beyond the jurisdiction of the people," who were "left in ignorance of what their servants are doing, and cannot protest against their acts until it is too late."

As an example, he put forth the case of a bill presented to pay a claim by the Carson City Sheriff, D.J. Gasherie. Bare-bones press accounts reported on that bill's success, yet readers were left in the dark as to what the claim was for — and how their tax money was being used. (Twain then revealed the bill appropriated $1,800 and $1,900 "for the maintenance by Sheriff Gasherie of several Ormsby County paupers.")

Moreover, without press scrutiny, lawmakers appeared poised to approve $50,000 for a private seminary and were about to purchase Abe Curry's hotel for $80,000 so they could have a permanent place to meet. Yet they were cool to another proposal to establish a public mining college.

The difference?

The first two projects were in Carson City; the third was in Storey County, home to Virginia City.

What happened to the American City bill? The fledgling town ultimately failed in its bid to secure the capital, but not by much. When the question was put to the assembly, it lost by just two votes.

Not to be discouraged, the town backed another bill the next year that would have separated Gold Hill and American City from Storey County, creating a new "Union County" around them.

American City in the early 1870s as photographed by Carleton Watkins, looking north toward Virginia City. *Joe Curtis Collection*

Getting to American City

The American Flats site is west of Nevada Route 342, midway between Silver City and Gold Hill. Nothing remains of the ghost town, and the 1920s mill that was built there has been demolished. The site is permanently closed.

This, too, failed.

American City, however, prospered — if only for a short time. Already in 1864-65 it boasted seven hotels, five saloons, and three grocery stores. A post office opened there in 1866.

The local mercantile guide spoke of the town in glowing terms: "The citizens have displayed an energy in building up this city that is not excelled by any body of people in the Territory... Buildings have been erected with such dispatch (and rapidly doubling in numbers) that the place now presents all the features of an old and well established city. Here can be found representatives of almost every trade, business, or profession...

"The site of the city has a natural location which is possessed by none of the neighboring cities. There are several springs which furnish sufficient water to supply the demands of a large city."

The town began to decline by 1867, although a new four-story cyanide mill was built there around 1920. It was closed six years later, however, and torn down as a hazard in 2014.

Two views of Aurora, where Samuel Clemens spent some time prospecting and, by his own account, nearly became a millionaire (see following pages). *Northeastern Nevada Museum and Historical Society*

Aurora.

By the time Aurora beckoned, Sam Clemens had already tried his luck, half-heartedly, at timber-cutting near Lake Tahoe, and he'd lived through the disappointment of a failed mining adventure in Unionville.

But he wasn't entirely disillusioned.

There were rich finds being made far closer to home than Humboldt County, and Clemens was "smitten with silver fever." He and his brother had bought up shares of mining companies in the Esmeralda Mining District, about 75 miles southeast of Carson City. He'd already taken a trip there back in September, and now his interest was renewed. At the heart of the district was a town later called Aurora, reportedly because of the magnificent glow of sunrises in the region.

Founded: **1860**
Location: **Esmeralda County**
Population (1863): **5,000**
Elevation: **7,441**
Status: **Abandoned**

Clemens was so gung-ho on his prospects there that he pulled up stakes and moved there in the spring of 1862 so he could personally see to his interests there.

Nearly four decades later, the *New York Times* would label

Aurora the site of "Mark Twain's First Success." Clemens was duly impressed with the town on his arrival and, according to the *Times*, "seemed to see in the town the makings of a great city," though it was a typical mining camp with "its rows of logwood saloons, its scattered cabins, its jail, and its church."

Founded in 1860, the town already had 1,400 residents just a year later, and a newspaper was founded there the year Clemens arrived. He took a hands-on approach, working as a miner digging and blasting tunnels on land where he had an interest "with the determination of a man who expects to see a twenty-pound nugget turn up with every thrust of the pick."

His efforts, alas, came to naught, and he earned his only regular income from a $10-a-week job working in a quartz mill.

Compensation included room and board, but it wasn't enough to live on, and he was forced to ask his brother for money to make ends meet.

In the meantime, Clemens amused himself by writing letters to the *Territorial Enterprise* in Virginia City under the pen name "Josh."

He later declared he was surprised to find they'd appeared in print.

Despite being unable to strike it rich in Aurora, Clemens hung around for a while, earning a reputation for his storytelling and, in consequence, being chosen to set the program for Aurora's Fourth of July celebration. He even wrote a speech for Mayor Leonard O. Stearns (who admitted he was unable to do so himself), which he sprinkled with humorous hyperbole such as: "I was sired by the great American eagle and born by a Continental dam."

The address concluded with more silly rhetoric, having the mayor claim that "the only mistake that Washington made was that he was not born in Aurora."

The crowd laughed heartily in response.

How much truth there was to Clemens' account of the speech is open to debate. Stearns did deliver a speech that day, but whether Clemens actually wrote the address he gave is unclear. His account, like some others, may have been embellished or invented out of whole cloth.

Regardless of whether it was actually delivered or not, the humorous speech wound up having repercussions far beyond Aurora.

It found its way onto the desk of Joseph T. Goodman, editor of the *Territorial Enterprise* in Virginia City, who wanted to publish it. Learning that Clemens was behind it, he wrote to the future Mark Twain with an offer of better compensation than he was probably getting as a miner: $25 a week.

Goodman could likely afford it. By 1863, he had built a staff of five editors and 23 printers, while the *Enterprise* was earning a cool $100,000 a year. (There was plenty of money to be made in the Comstock, even if you weren't a miner.)

Clemens didn't answer the letter, but instead simply left Aurora, writing a bitter missive to his brother in which he declared it "the damnedest country for disappointments the world ever saw." Shortly thereafter, he arrived at the *Enterprise* office carrying nothing more than a roll of dirty blankets, which he dropped on the floor with a shrug. Thus began his tenure as a journalist in Nevada and his renewed career as a writer.

Cramped quarters

While he wasn't in Aurora long, Clemens lived in not one but as many as three different mining cabins during his time there. He first moved in with Horatio "Ratio" Phillips, a friend he'd met at a political convention in Carson City.

The partnership didn't last, though.

Of Phillips, he later wrote: "He is a damned rascal, and I can get the signatures of 25 men to this sentiment whenever I want them."

Sam Clemens and Calvin Higbie in their Aurora cabin, as depicted in *Roughing It*.

Their friendship severed, Twain moved out of Phillips' cabin and in with next-door neighbor Calvin H. Higbie, but found conditions there to be far from ideal: "I have no private room, and it is a torture to write when there is a crowd around, as it is the case here always."

The dwelling, at the base of a mountain called Lover's Leap, was as much a tent as a cabin: Its log siding supported a canvas roof. Just 11 feet square, it made for "very cramped quarters, with barely room for us and the stove," Clemens recalled. Other than that, furnishings consisted of the stove and two beds separated by a simple wooden table.

The temperature inside would vary wildly: "Now and then, between eight in the morning and eight in the evening, the thermometer would make an excursion of 50 degrees."

Unlike his brief association with Phillips, however, Clemens' friendship with Higbie proved to be enduring. He even dedicated his book *Roughing It* to Higbie, whom he called "an honest man, a genial comrade, and a steadfast friend."

Clemens also apparently lived in a third Aurora cabin, this one owned by a man named Robert Howland on the west end of town, below the China Garden district.

Millionaires for Ten Days

But it was in the company of Higbie that Clemens very nearly struck it rich at Aurora.

Higbie had come across a "blind lead" going through the Wide West vein near the top of Last Chance Hill. A blind lead was a ledge that didn't crop out at the surface. Suspecting the presence of such a lead, Higbie had snuck into the Wide West mine through a side shaft to confirm its presence.

The Wide West Company, a significant player in Aurora which spent $150,000 to build 20-stamp mill built in 1862, had rights to the vein. But the blind lead wasn't part of it: It cut through the Wide West vein diagonally, enclosed in its own "well-defined casing of rocks and clay." As a result, the Wide West Company didn't own it. It was, in fact, on public property, just waiting to be claimed.

Higbie and Clemens were ready to do just that along with a third partner, Wide West foreman A.D. Allen: "We are going to take possession of this blind lead, record it and establish ownership, and then forbid the Wide West company to take out any more of the rock," Higbie declared.

They went to the recorder, registered their claim and started dreaming of becoming millionaires with lavish homes in San Francisco and enough money to travel around Europe.

Clemens and Higbie celebrate their good fortune in this illustration from *Roughing It*.

But then they let it all slip through their fingers.

Rather than staying in town to safeguard their find, both Clemens and Higbie absented themselves from the site. As fate would have it, Clemens had received word that a good friend of his — "Captain" John Nye — had fallen gravely ill with rheumatism at his Nine-Mile Ranch. (Nye was the brother of James Nye, the territorial governor, for whom Nye County is named.)

In response, Clemens made plans to visit the ranch and help Nye's wife care for him. Thinking Higbie was at the cabin,

Clemens ran there to tell him of those plans, but Higbie wasn't there, so he left a note.

Higbie never saw it.

He had left town, too, abruptly, taking the word of one Gid Whiteman (a prospector with whom he was acquainted) that he was on the verge of locating the so-called Lost Cement Mine near Mono Lake. Unfortunately, their search came up empty, and while Higbie and Clemens were away, others began conspiring to wrest their Aurora claim away from them.

Under local ordinance, a claim was considered abandoned if the owners hadn't done enough work to show they were developing it. Since Higbie and Clemens had both been out of town, they hadn't satisfied that condition. So at midnight on the 10th day, a crowd of "duly armed" men converged on their blind lead with the intention of claiming it as their own under the name of Johnson.

Only Clemens' other partner, Allen, got there in time to contest the claim-jumpers' action. Armed with a revolver, he threatened to "thin out the Johnson company some," unless they added his name to the list of owners. Duly persuaded, they acceded to his demand, and he got a stake; Clemens and Higbie, however, were left out in the cold.

"We would have been millionaires," Clemens lamented, "if we had only worked with pick and spade one little day on our property and so secured our ownership!"

Indeed, the Johnson claim wound up producing millions of dollars in gold and silver. The newly formed company soon merged with the existing Wide West firm, while Allen took the money and ran: He sold his share for $90,000 in gold and went home to enjoy it.

Clemens, meanwhile, was left to write about the unfortunate

turn of events in *Roughing It*, which he dedicated to Higbie "in memory of the curious time when we two were millionaires for ten days."

Battle for the Border

While Clemens soon left Aurora, others stayed behind, certain they would make a killing from the mines there — although they weren't exactly sure where "there" was.

Were they in California? Or Nevada?

In fact, both states claimed jurisdiction over the town: The year before Clemens arrived (1861), California had designated it as the seat of Mono County. Nevada, in a case of tit-for-tat, responded by naming it the seat of Esmeralda County.

In March of that year, California paid a surveyor $10,000 to locate the proper boundary. In November, Nevada set aside $1,000 of its own to accomplish the same task.

Nothing came of either action, however, and the dispute refused to die.

Until 1863, residents could actually vote in both states: Nevadans could vote Democrat in the general store, while pro-Union Californians could vote Republican across the street at the saloon.

The *Esmeralda Star* newspaper threw in its own two cents, supporting California's case. It was better, the *Star* reasoned, for Aurora to be located in a full-fledged state than within the boundary of a mere territory.

In an editorial, the *Star* declared: "The young suckling, Mono County, which has drawn its full milk from the breasts of the parent state of California, will hardly like to turn to the dry nurse of Nevada Territory which has not yet been admitted into the family of married states, and brought to her milk."

Complicating matters was the fact that the Esmeralda Mining District had been incorporated under the laws of California.

Both sides were making a major push to claim Aurora. The situation had become all the more pressing in February, when a similar conflict between Plumas County in California and Nevada's Roop County over Honey Lake Valley became so heated that both sides took up arms. Judge John Roop holed up with 30 men in a log fort he'd built a decade earlier to defend against Native American attacks. A brief battle ensued, in which a couple of people were injured, but four hours later, it was all over.

Cooler heads eventually prevailed, and a joint committee sent delegations to both state capitals to plead their cases. Governor Leland Stanford received them in California; in Nevada, the task would naturally have fallen to the governor, James Nye. But Nye was away at the time, so the duty fell to the acting governor.

Secretary Orion Clemens.

In the end, surveyors determined that most of the land was in California, and the sliver of Roop County that was left wasn't big enough to continue on its own. Instead, it was eventually annexed to neighboring Washoe County (although Roop's fort still stands in Susanville, and there's a Roop Street in Carson City).

Such difficulties may have forced California and Nevada to play nice so as to avoid a similar violent outburst over Aurora. So, in April of 1863, California lawmakers commissioned a survey "to establish the eastern boundary of the state of California" and, as a courtesy, decided to request the governor of Nevada to join the survey." A joint boundary commission was formed, with California's surveyor-general appointing a man named John Kidder to represent that state.

Orion Clemens, in his position as acting governor, appointed Butler Ives to the task.

Ives was up by Lake Tahoe at the time, doing a survey there that had implications for Aurora: His team determined that the "angle" of the state line changed at the southeast corner of the lake, no longer running from north to south but heading south by southeast from that point on.

This determination put Aurora on Nevada's side of the line, a conclusion supported by the joint survey party in late September, around the autumn equinox. Aurora was in Nevada, and in Nevada it would stay.

Boom Goes Bust

By that time, Aurora was a full-fledged boomtown with 20 stores, 22 saloons and 760 houses. There was a blacksmith's shop, brewery, stable, and slaughterhouse, and the crude miner's shacks were gradually being replaced by more permanent structures. A year later, the population had swollen to 6,000.

There was even a two-story hotel, which had been built as a courthouse on the assumption that Aurora was in California, but which was converted into lodging after Nevada took over. (The seat of Mono County was moved to Bridgeport at that point.)

But as with so many boomtowns, the bust was soon to follow. The town had churned out $27 million worth of gold by 1869 and was, at one point, home to 17 mills. But seven of them had already shut down by 1864, and production continued to sag.

By 1870, the town was clearly on the decline, but a slow decline it was.

Top: Aurora around 1910 still had some life to it, but nothing like the feverish activity that was taking place during Sam Clemens' day.
Above: Aurora's main street was deserted in 1934, and its buildings were crumbling. *Historic American Buildings Survey*

The 1880 census showed just 341 residents living there, and that figure had dropped to 225 by 1890.

There were 75 people still living there at the turn of the century, and a few more (93) in 1910, when an odd photograph shows buildings still standing and a number of men hanging idly about in front of places with names like the Tunnel and Northern saloons. Two men and a young boy stand on one streetcorner, apparently performing as a three-piece drum band.

That was the last gasp for Aurora, however, with the 1920 census finding just six residents, and none remaining to be counted after that. More than 100 ruins lined its deserted streets in the 1940s.

One man still lived in Aurora in 1944: Fred Walker, a native of Switzerland who had arrived in 1905.

Aurora, or what was left of it, in the 1940s. *U.S. Forest Service*

Getting to Aurora

U.S. 395 — Take Nevada Route 208 east to NR 338 south
U.S. 95 — Take NR 395 east to NFD Trail 058 north
4-wheel-drive recommended

Austin.

Prospectors were always looking for the next big vein, and in 1862, they found one.

While Sam Clemens was in Virginia City, William Talcott was discovering silver ore more than 150 miles to the east in the Toiyabe Mountains. This led to the founding of two towns: Clifton and nearby Austin, with the latter quickly becoming a boomtown.

Founded: **1862**
Location: **Lander County**
Population (1863): **10,000**
Elevation: **6,575**
Status: **Semi-ghost town**

Just a year after the initial find in Pony Canyon, Austin was crawling with prospectors and men eager to make money off them. Its population soared to 7,000 in 1863, and the new settlement was such big news that the owners of the International Hotel in Virginia City picked it up and physically moved it all the way there.

Mark Twain wrote of the sensation surrounding Austin in the July 1 edition of the *Enterprise*. "When Dan De Quille passed along there, less than six months ago, there were probably not a dozen white men in that part of America," he recalled.

The International Hotel still stands today in Austin. Originally built in Virginia City, a portion of it was moved to Austin when that town started booming. *Author photo*

Much had changed in those six months.

"At the present moment, next to our own section of Washoe, Reese River occupies the most prominent position before the speculative San Francisco eye. Esmeralda and Humboldt have had their day of excitements, and have settled down into the comfortable dog trot of acknowledged worth and secured independence, but Reese River has only recently begun to blaze."

Mills were going up left and right (nine in all, by Twain's count) to process the ore, one of which was planned by Judge Hall of Carson City. Hall went to Austin, Twain reported, to sign a $40,000 contract for a 20-stamp mill to be built between Clifton and Austin.

Gridley's Crusade

One of the people who found his way there was Reuel Colt "R.C." Gridley, a veteran of the Mexican-American War who'd gone to school with Sam Clemens back in Hannibal, Missouri. He started up a general store in Austin and, when the town incorporated in 1864, decided to run for mayor as a Democrat.

As a friendly wager, Gridley bet his opponent — Republican Dr. H.S. Herrick — concerning the outcome of the election: Whoever won would present the loser with a 50-pound sack of flour, which he would have to carry on his shoulder from Clinton to Austin. If Herrick won, Gridley would have to march to the tune of "John Brown's Body," and if Gridley won, Herrick would be obliged to carry the sack while a band played "Dixie."

Gridley was defeated, but he wasn't a sore loser. When presented with the flour sack, he made good on his promise and hoisted it onto his shoulder, then carried it thorough town. Everyone turned out to watch the spectacle, and Gridley marched a mile or two through town, accompanied by music from a brass band.

When he was done, he asked what he should do with the flour.

Someone suggested that he sell it at auction and give the proceeds to the Sanitary Fund, a Civil War charity for sick and wounded soldiers founded in 1861 that served as a forerunner of the Red Cross. Gridley did so, but when he sought to deliver it, the high bidder said he didn't want it.

So he sold it again.

And again.

And again.

In fact, he sold it 300 times without ever parting with the flour, raising some $8,000 in gold in the process.

When news of these developments reached Virginia City, the folks there invited Gridley to town for more flour-sack sales. An auction was held at Maguire's Opera House, and $5,000 was raised initially, with the figure eventually rising to $13,000.

Next up was Gold Hill. The Metropolitan

R.C. Gridley and his flour sack.

Brass Band, a carriage filled with reporters, and a group of citizens on foot all made their way down there, stopping in front of Maynard's Bank for another auction. There the Yellow Jacket Mining Company opened the bidding at $1,000, and the town collected a total of $6,600.

Gridley's campaign (known as "The Army of the Lord") continued from there, with Silver City pitching in $1,800, and Dayton pledging slightly more. Gridley then took his sack and went on tour to California, racking up more proceeds in Auburn, Placerville, Grass Valley, Marysville, and Sacramento.

Twain kept a tally of the totals, rewarding each local contributor with a mention in his reporting for the *Territorial Enterprise*. Things were going so well that he estimated the total might go beyond $500,000 if the major cities did their part. (He suggested that San Francisco, Boston, Chicago, Cincinnati, and St. Louis might give $50,000 apiece, with New York and Philadelphia each pitching in $100,000.)

Being from Missouri himself, Twain naturally touted the St. Louis Fair as a potential source of funds for his childhood friend's charitable effort.

"Now supposing that the managers of the St. Louis Fair are smart enough to have this historical sack of flour ultimately made into thin wafer cakes — 500 to the pound," he mused. "It strikes us that 25,000 people would willingly give $5 a cake for it, if only for the sake of telling their children and friends that they had eaten a cake made out of flour that had sold for over $500,000 per sack! This would add $125,000 to the receipts, making the total amount received upon the 50-pound sack of Sanitary flour swell to the enormous sum of $671,610!"

Twain's estimate turned out to be generous, but the campaign — which covered 15,000 miles — still racked up an impressive $275,000 in donations.

Leaving Nevada

Twain was no doubt happy to help an old friend, but unfortunately, his cheerleading of Gridley's efforts brought him nothing but trouble. In the end, it cost him his job at the *Enterprise*, and he left Nevada for San Francisco, having been challenged to a pair of duels as a result.

Everything came to a head on a week when Twain was left in charge of the *Territorial Enterprise* while his boss, Joe Goodman, was away. Twain later recalled the effects of the added responsibility on him: "It destroyed me."

In over his head and unable to find a subject to write about, Twain frittered away his time and produced material by copying a pair of articles out of an encyclopedia.

Meanwhile, the big news continued to be Gridley's charity efforts. Everyone seemed to be getting into the act. In Carson City, a ladies' aid group held a "Fancy Dress Ball," at which they repeatedly auctioned off a sack of flour to benefit the Sanitary Fund. Twain, focused as he was on supporting the St. Louis Fair efforts, got it in his head that the ladies' aid funds were being delivered to the fair organizers there. Instead, however, they had been sent to the national Sanitary Commission.

Thinking some nefarious plot was afoot to siphon off funds destined for the charity, Twain lashed out in a fit of sarcasm, charging that the money had been "diverted from its legitimate course, and was to be sent to aid a Miscegenation Society somewhere in the East."

His charge that the money was being used to promote interracial marriage was entirely baseless (not to mention racist). Being falsely accused, the women who'd organized the event had every reason to be livid — and they were.

They penned a blunt letter to the editor in response, stating that "the ladies in charge consider themselves capable of deciding as to what shall be done with the money, without the aid of outsiders, who are probably desirous of acquiring some glory by appropriating the efforts of the ladies themselves."

Twain, in his position as acting chief editor, refused to print the letter. It showed up instead — three days in a row — in the rival *Virginia Union*, which Twain had challenged to a competition over which paper would donate more to the Sanitary Fund.

When the *Union* outbid the *Enterprise*, Twain was left looking like a fool.

Amidst all this turmoil, the ladies' aid group responded to Twain's false accusations by expelling Mollie Clemens, his sister-in-law, from their membership. Not only did this make Twain look bad, it reflected poorly on his brother Orion, the territorial secretary, who was serving as acting governor at the time. With their only child, Jennie, having died of meningitis earlier that year, the affront was especially difficult to bear.

Twain wrote to Mollie, dismissing his own criticism of the ladies' efforts as "a silly joke" concocted when he was drunk. He claimed that he'd left the manuscript lying on the table at the *Enterprise* office before he and colleague Dan De Quille left for the theater. The foreman, seeing it there, assumed that since his boss had written it, it was meant to be published.

"Since it has made the ladies angry," he wrote, "I am sorry the thing occurred."

It was a half-hearted apology at best, and it did nothing to assuage the wrath of the ladies' aid leaders. The group's president, Ellen Cutler, told her husband about it, and he promptly defended her honor by challenging Twain to a duel.

He wasn't the only one.

Twain's sparring with the *Virginia Union* escalated when he lashed out at its owner and editor, James Laird, in an editorial accusing his newspaper of refusing to honor its Sanitary Fund pledge. Perhaps he was trying to save face; perhaps he was just miffed.

Either way, the *Union* responded with a piece written by one J.W. Wilmington (a printer at the Union who'd previously been an owner of the *Cincinnati Enquirer*) that accused Twain of cowardice and "unmanly public journalism," denouncing him as "a liar, a poltroon and a puppy."

Twain sent a letter demanding a retraction.

Wilmington refused: "I have nothing to retract."

Twain then sent another letter to Laird, demanding "the satisfaction due a gentleman — without alternative."

In other words, a duel.

There was precedent for this. The previous summer, then-*Union* editor Thomas Fitch had challenged Goodman to a duel over an insulting article he had written (but not yet published). The challenge was accepted. According to Twain, reporting in the *Enterprise*, the duel "with navy revolvers at fifteen paces," was ready to begin when police interfered to prevent it. But according to another version of the story, the duel was actually held. Goodman found out that Fitch didn't know how to use a gun, so he shot him below the knee to avoid killing him.

Now, Twain faced a similar showdown with Fitch's successor, but Laird wasn't as eager to settle the issue as Fitch had been. In answer to Twain, he replied that Wilmington had first claim on such a showdown, but added that "when he is through with you, I shall be at your service."

Twain accused Laird of trying to hide his "craven carcass" behind Wilmington.

And so it went.

The back-and-forth continued, with Twain publishing the entire exchange (seven letters in all) in the pages of the *Enterprise*.

Twain prepared to defend his honor by squaring off against whoever wanted to face him and enlisted fellow *Enterprise* journalist Stephen Gillis to be his second in any duel. In the end, however, the threats and insults proved to be bluster on all sides. Goodman returned to find Twain's resignation waiting for him and, in Twain's inflated recollection, "six duels on his hands."

But no duel ever took place.

In his autobiography, Twain related a colorful story about

having agreed to square off against Laird around sunrise, at 5 in the morning. In preparation, he had Gillis set up a fence rail against a barn door and practiced shooting at it. The rail, Twain said, served as a suitable stand-in for Laird, who was "longer than a rail and thinner."

Twain, however, not only failed to hit the rail, he missed the barn door altogether.

Gillis, on the other hand, was both a tough guy (despite weighing just 95 pounds) and a marksman. Upon seeing a sparrow fly past and land in the sagebrush, he reportedly shot its head off from 30 yards away. As luck would happen, Laird happened along at precisely this moment and asked who'd fired the shot.

"Clemens did it," Gillis responded.

Laird, shaken, withdrew from the agreement and sent a note refusing to take part in a duel with Twain "on any terms whatever."

Austin in the early days. *Northeastern Nevada Museum*

That left the dispute with Cutler to be resolved. Ellen Cutler's husband had just come into town from Carson City, and had sent a man to Twain with a challenge. At this point, Twain wrote, he wasn't eager to participate in an actual duel because he'd received a warning from Justice John North of the territorial supreme court that he would face two years in prison if he violated a law against the practice.

Flour Sacks

R.C. Gridley wasn't the only person to carry a sack of flour around this time — although P.H. Clayton did so for a very different reason. Clayton, an attorney and Confederate sympathizer, was arrested for presumably "uttering treasonable language." After his arrest, he was taken to Fort Churchill. (*Sacramento Daily Union*)

A sign beside Clayton's grave at Lone Mountain Cemetery says he carried a 100-pound sack of flour around the parade grounds during a three-week sentence at Fort Churchill, apparently as punishment for being a "notorious" secessionist. A founding member of the Nevada Democratic Party, he served with the Carson Rangers during the Pyramid Lake War.

He therefore sent Gillis down to the local hotel, where Cutler was staying, to confront him. Gillis, according to Twain, had a reputation for being able to "whip anybody that walked on two legs." So it was natural that, when Cutler saw him coming, "he became calm and rational, and was ready to listen."

Above: Reuel Gridley's store went belly-up when he went on his flour-sack charity tour, but the building still stands in Austin today. *Author photo*

Right: Sanitary Commission seal, as shown in *Roughing It.*

Gillis gave him half an hour to get out of town, and Cutler obliged, returning to Carson.

How much truth there is to Twain's account is uncertain. What is known is that he did, in fact, quit the *Enterprise* and leave Nevada altogether, traveling to San Francisco before the month was out.

Gridley, meanwhile, continued on his tour, but it cost him all the money he'd made from the silver boom, and he returned to

Getting to Austin

U.S. 50 — Austin is accessible from east or west via U.S. 50.
NR 376 — Take Nevada Route 376 north from Tonopah.

Austin in 1865 to find his store had gone belly-up. Broke and in poor health, he moved to California to live with his sister in Stockton. He passed away a few years later in Stanislaus County at the age of 41.

Early scene on Austin's main street. *Northeastern Nevada Museum*

Austin's fortunes, similarly, declined as the silver boom there waned. The population in 1880 was 1,679, but more than a quarter of those residents had departed a decade later, the last time the census recorded it topping 1,000.

Perhaps the decisive blow came when the Manhattan Silver Mining Company went out of business in 1897.

The seat of Lander County for more than a century, Austin lost that title when it was transferred to Battle Mountain in 1979. As of 2020, it was a semi-ghost town with just 167 residents.

As for nearby Clifton, nothing but the ruins of an old mill remained there.

Key Sites in Austin

Gridley Store — 247 Water St. at Reese St., just north of 50
International Hotel — 59 Main St. (U.S. 50)

Bodie, California.

Aurora was just about 12 miles from another famous boomtown, Bodie, just on the other side of the California state line.

Bodie had been founded in 1859, a year before Aurora, when a man named W.S. Bodey and some companions discovered gold there.

Founded: **1859**
Location: **Mono County, Calif.**
Population (1880): **10,000**
Elevation: **8,379**
Status: **Ghost town/state park**

Sam Clemens' cabin in Aurora with Calvin Higbie fronted Spring Street, which ran through town and continued west all the way to Bodie. Clemens must have spent a little time there, for he commented on its climate (derisively) as "the breakup of one winter and the beginning of the next."

"It was a plain wonder," he said, "how man carried on under such circumstances."

The winters were so harsh there, in fact, that founder Bodey died in a blizzard a year after the town was established. Average low temperatures are in single digits all winter and below freezing 10 months out of the year.

Scenes from Bodie in 2022.
Unlike Aurora, it is
remarkably well-preserved.
Author photos

Bodie as it appeared around 1890.

Considering the conditions, there wasn't much to attract fortune-seekers to Bodie, where the prospecting was meager throughout the 1860s. (Only two companies built stamp mills, and both had gone out of business by 1868.)

It wasn't until a richer vein of gold was discovered in 1876 that Bodie started booming, several years after Aurora was tapped out.

Like Aurora, Bodie was practically deserted by the mid-20th century. Earl Bell was the only remaining resident there — a summer resident, at that — in 1959. You could still see the outlines of the old Bodie baseball diamond at that point, long since vanished now. As for Aurora, Bell said it wasn't worth the trip.

"You don't want to go there," he told a reporter. "The whole town's been highgraded."

That was his way of saying it had been picked apart by

vandals, many of whom had taken the bricks from Aurora's abandoned structures to San Francisco, Reno, and Las Vegas, to use in buildings there. There had been 100 ruins in Aurora a decade or so earlier, but they had mostly disappeared.

Today, there's barely anything left in Aurora, but Bodie is a remarkably well-preserved ghost towns thanks to its status as a state park in California.

Getting to Bodie

U.S. 395 — Take California State Route 270 east from 395 to Bodie. The last 10 miles is gravel road, but 4-wheel-drive is not necessary.

Carson City.

Samuel Clemens wasn't the most famous person in Nevada, or even in his own family, when he arrived in the new territorial capital.

His first impressions of the place were hardly glowing:

"It was a 'wooden' town," he later observed, "its population two thousand souls. The main street consisted of four or five blocks of little white frame stores which were too high to sit down on, but not too high for various other purposes; in fact, hardly high enough. They were packed close together, side by side, as if room were scarce in that mighty plain.

Founded: **1858**
Location: **Ormsby County***
Population (1860): **714****
Elevation: **4,802**
Status: **State capital**

Now Carson City County
** *2020 population: 58,639*

"The sidewalk was of boards that were more or less loose and inclined to rattle when walked upon. In the middle of the town, opposite the stores, was the 'plaza' which is native to all towns beyond the Rocky Mountains — a large, unfenced, level vacancy, with a liberty pole in it, and very useful as a place for public auctions, horse trades, and mass meetings, and likewise for teamsters to camp in. Two other sides of the plaza were faced by stores, offices and stables."

These were the scenes that confronted Sam Clemens when he pulled into town in 1861 along with his older brother. Orion

Views of Carson Street in 1863, with the Ormsby House (closeup directly above) at right in top photo.

was making the trip because he'd accepted a position as secretary of Nevada Territory, which had been carved out of Utah in March of that year. The position, to which he was appointed by no less a personage than President Abe Lincoln, paid $1,800, which was enough incentive for the ambitious Orion to move west.

The younger Clemens, meanwhile, had a different motive: He wanted to avoid any further involvement in the Civil War, and may have viewed the Western frontier as a haven from a conflict he later described as "a blot on our history, but not as great a blot as the buying and selling of Negro souls."

It was the war that had brought an end to Sam Clemens' career as a steamboat pilot on the Mississippi in 1861 by interrupting the flow of goods up and down the river. Out of work and ignorant, by his own account, of the politics behind the war, he had joined a Confederate militia called the Marion Rangers.

That endeavor came to a halt after just two short weeks. Clemens' somewhat fictionalized account of those two weeks depicts a disorganized band of untrained, undisciplined young men who acted more like the Keystone Cops than a military force. In one comedic incident, a member of the group carrying a powder keg lost his footing on a muddy slope and tumbled all the way to the bottom, carrying the entire detachment with him.

His involvement ended when, according to Clemens, news arrived in their camp that a Union regiment led by Ulysses S. Grant was bearing down on them. The militia members held a meeting and determined that "the war was a disappointment for us and we were going to disband."

Half of the 15 Rangers quit then and there. They ran into Brigadier General Thomas Harris on the road after that, and he tried to order them back — but the spooked deserters were in no mood to be ordered around. Harris "raged a little bit, but it was of no use," and the group continued on their way back home.

That summer, at the age of 25, Clemens hightailed it out of Missouri and went west to Nevada with his brother, ostensibly to serve as his elder sibling's assistant (though he did little work in that capacity). But he was soon disabused of any romantic illusions that he may have had about the brave new world on the frontier. It was no Shangri-La. On the contrary it was a desolate and forbidding country.

"It never rains here, and the dew never falls. No flowers grow here, and no green thing gladdens the eye," he wrote in a letter to his mother. "The birds that fly over the land carry their provisions with them. Only the crow and the raven tarry with us."

Capital Projects

Orion Clemens was an important man in Carson City, but he was hardly the prime mover and shaker.

The big man in town was Abraham Curry, who would serve as first superintendent of the Carson Mint, first warden of the Nevada State Prison, and builder of the Virginia & Truckee Railroad machine shop and engine house in Carson City.

The Ohio businessman had been rebuffed when he tried to settle in Genoa, so he headed to Eagle Valley instead. Curry had arrived with a couple of men he'd met in Utah — Frank Proctor and John Musser, both of whom have streets named after them in Carson City. He'd offered $1,000 for a 900-acre lot in Genoa, the region's first settlement, but had been turned down.

Abraham Curry built the V&T Railroad Shops, seen here in 1972 from the west side looking southeast between Plaza, Ann, and Stewart streets. The shops have since been demolished. *Historic American Buildings Survey*

The Territorial Governor's House in Carson City during Samuel Clemens' time, as seen in *Roughing It*.

Abraham Curry built the Warm Springs Hotel on the site of the future Nevada State Prison. Curry sold the state land for the prison and served as its first warden.

Undeterred by his Genoa setback, Curry procured some land in Carson, where he built a couple of hotels: the Great Basin and the Warm Springs. Both were significant in the nascent history of Nevada. In 1862, Curry sold the Great Basin to the state for $42,500 so it could be used as the new courthouse.

It contained the county jail, and church services were held there, too, on Sundays. As Twain reported for the *Territorial Enterprise*, he attended a service there in February of 1863.

"By an easy and pleasant transition, I went from church to jail," he wrote. "It was only just down stairs — for they save men eternally in the second story of the new court house, and damn them for life in the first."

His description of the courthouse was characteristically colorful: "Sheriff Gasherie has a handsome double office fronting on the street, and its walls are gorgeously decorated with iron convict-jewelry. In the rear are two rows of cells, built of bombproof masonry and furnished with strong iron doors and resistless locks and bolts.

"There was but one prisoner — Swayze, the murderer of Derickson — and he was writing; I do not know what his subject was, but he appeared to be handling it in a way which gave him great satisfaction..."

A year after Curry sold the Great Basin, Carson became a Pony Express stop, with a telegraph line connecting it to San Francisco. Genoa Mayor William Ormsby, who opened a hotel of his own (called the Ormsby House) in Carson City, threw his weight behind the effort to get Curry's fledgling town named the territorial capital as well as the seat of a new county, also named for Ormsby.

Curry's Warm Springs Hotel, meanwhile, was used as the first meeting place for the Territorial Legislature, while the second and third sessions met at the former Great Basin. Curry pocketed $80,000 more when he sold land near the Warm Springs Hotel to the state so it could be used for the Nevada State Prison. Curry, conveniently enough, became the first warden.

Twain for Governor

In the fall of 1863, Twain was assigned to cover the First Territorial Constitutional Convention in Carson City. He traveled back and forth between Virginia City and the capital, where he sometimes stayed at the home of his brother, Orion.

Twain, however, presided over an alternative version of the legislature known as the Third House — a takeoff on the term "Fourth Estate," often used to describe journalism (the other three being the three recognized branches of government: executive, legislative, and judicial.)

Orion Clemens' home in Carson City, as seen in 1935 and 2022.
*University of Southern California Libraries and California Historical
Society (top); author photo*

Since there were two houses in the legislature, the name "Third House" was chosen for the satirical group to which Twain belonged. Its purpose was to lampoon the legislature, but it was all in good fun: Meetings were held after the legislative sessions were done for the day, so the lawmakers themselves could attend.

Twain was elected president of the group in December and named governor of its mock territorial convention, and in January of 1864, he was scheduled to speak to the group at a benefit for the First Presbyterian Church of Carson City.

Twain would later make a name for himself not only as a writer, but as a public speaker, but he had a case of stage fright on the occasion of his first public address, as shown in this illustration from *Roughing It.*

Twain wasn't a churchgoer, but his brother was a founding member, and Orion's daughter Jennie was raising money for a pulpit Bible at the church. (Jennie sadly contracted spotted fever and died before all the money was raised, but women at the church donated the balance of what was needed in her name, and the Bible they purchased in her memory is on display at the church today. By 2011, it was the oldest continuously operating church in Nevada.)

Above: First Presbyterian Church in Carson City, built in 1864 with funds from Mark Twain's speech.

Left: Pulpit Bible Jennie Clemons helped purchase. *Author photos*

Twain therefore consented to "willingly inflict my annual message upon the church itself if it might derive benefit thereby."

Whether that was a compliment or an insult, and, if the latter, whether it was directed at Twain himself or the church (or both) wasn't exactly clear. But it probably wasn't supposed to be. Twain liked to keep people guessing about the truth of matters, as had already been evident for some time at this point. And such a response was entirely in keeping with the satirical spirit of the Third House.

It was Twain's first public address, and he was, understandably, nervous.

"I delivered that message last night," he wrote the following day, "but I didn't talk loud enough — people at the far end of the hall could not hear me. They said, 'Louder-louder,' occasionally, but I thought that was the way they had — a joke, as it were. I had never talked to a crowd before, and knew none of the tactics of a public speaker... Some folks heard the entire document, though — there is some comfort in that."

Twain's address raised $200 for the church's building fund, and the sanctuary was completed in May of that year.

Twain, for his part, received a $200 gold watch as a gift to "His Excellency Governor Twain," which he judged to be "a pretty good result for an oratorial slouch like me, isn't it?"

In Stages

Another man of some importance in Carson City was someone Twain said he'd heard quite enough about, thank you very much.

In Twain's day, there were a few ways to get around: You could take the train, you could ride a horse, you could walk... or you could take the stage. But a stagecoach wasn't like a modern car, where you did the driving. Either you were wealthy enough to own one, in which case you paid someone else to drive, or you were NOT wealthy enough to own one — which also meant you paid someone else to take the reins.

Driving wasn't something you generally did yourself. If you needed to get around in town, most places were in walking distance, and roads outside of town were bad to non-existent.

The government didn't pay for them back then, which meant any upkeep had to be undertaken by private companies, which needed a reason to maintain them.

That meant they needed to make a profit, which is why roads between towns (such as they were) were toll roads back then.

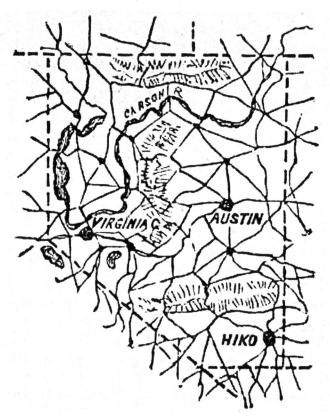

Stage drivers traveled between towns by toll roads in Twain's day, as this map from *Roughing It* illustrates.

"Maintained" didn't mean "paved." Roads weren't paved back then. At best, they were gravel, and that was rare enough. Generally, if you wanted to get where you were going on those rutted, rock-strewn, often washed-out trails, you didn't want to be the one driving. You'd need someone who knew both where he was going and how to get there in one piece.

Stage lines employed men who knew how to do just that.

Virginia City's mercantile guide boasted in 1864 that there was "perhaps no city in the United States, and there is certainly none on the Pacific coast, that can boast of as many stage lines radiating from her limits as Virginia."

The Overland Stage Company delivered the U.S. mail daily between Sacramento and the Missouri River, but that was just the beginning. Some companies offered local travel, and others could drive you across the Sierra.

Locally, W.F. Wilson's Accommodation Line had a reputation for keeping its stages and horses in excellent condition under the personal supervision of owner "Billy" Wilson, whose reputation was well known across the region (at least according to the Virginia City mercantile guide).

Wilson's line could take you between Virginia City and Carson, leaving for the capital at 2:30 each afternoon and departing in the opposite direction at 9 each morning. Langton's Pioneer Express, which Twain mentioned using, offered similar service in the morning from Virginia at 9:30 and in the afternoon from Carson at 2. It also carried passengers and mail between Virginia and Unionville in Humboldt County.

Crandall's Pioneer Omnibus Line ran between Virginia and Gold Hill, while Russell & Co. operated between Virginia and Dayton, each offering daily service. Another line offered daily stages between Virginia City and Steamboat Springs.

For longer trips, you could choose the Pacific Stage Company, which traveled to Sacramento via Truckee and Auburn along the Dutch Flat and Donner Lake Toll Road. Steamboats could take you from Sacramento on to San Francisco. The California Stage Company, one of the oldest on the Pacific Coast, took the same route, approximating today's Interstate 80.

But you could also choose the Pioneer Stage Line if you wanted to travel the southern route, which took you down to Carson City, Genoa, and Placerville to Sacramento, along what was then known as Johnson Pass Road and was later replaced by U.S. Highway 50.

Hank Monk lived in the St. Charles Hotel, seen here in 2022. His employer, the Pioneer Stage Line, had its offices there. *Author photo*

The Pioneer company boasted one of the best drivers in the business: Hank Monk, who lived at the St. Charles Hotel in Carson City. His choice of residence wasn't accidental: The Pioneer Line had its offices at the St. Charles, erected in 1862 right across the street from where the Pony Express had corralled its horses two years earlier.

The St. Charles, which still stands on Carson Street today (in Nevada, only the Gold Hill Hotel is older), was a popular hangout for state lawmakers and had the requisite bar on the ground floor. Given Mark Twain's beat covering the legislature and his taste for liquor, those twin facts make it likely that he spent some time there.

Twain made at least one trip on the stage line with Monk and was present at an 1863 ceremony in Carson, where Monk was presented with "a superb gold watch, worth five or six hundred dollars."

"Champagne flowed freely," he reported in the *Territorial Enterprise*, describing the watch as "gorgeously embellished with coaches and horses, and with charms and seals in keeping with the same." It also bore a quotation from Monk to perhaps his most famous passenger, *New York Tribune* editor and 1872 presidential candidate Horace Greeley: "Keep your seat, Horace. I'll get you there on time."

Twain knew that story well — so well, in fact, that he got tired of hearing it. It seemed to be on everyone's lips. On his trip west to Carson City in 1861, Twain recalled hearing the same anecdote from no fewer than five different people. He therefore repeated it five times, verbatim for comic effect, in *Roughing It*.

One day in 1859, Greeley enlisted Monk's services to convey him from Carson City to Placerville, where he was to deliver a lecture, and wanted to be sure he got there on time. Monk took the charge seriously: too seriously for Greeley's wellbeing.

Twain continues:

"Hank Monk cracked his whip and started off at an awful pace. The coach bounced up and down in such a terrific way that it jolted the buttons all off of Horace's coat, and finally shot his head clean through the roof of the stage, and then he yelled at Hank Monk and begged him to go easier — said he warn't in as much of a hurry as he was awhile ago."

Illustration of Greeley's ride from *Roughing It.*

That's when Monk supposedly uttered his famous phrase, later inscribed on the watch, "Keep your seat, Horace. I'll get you there on time."

"And you bet he did, too," the story concluded, "what was left of him."

Getting to Carson City

I-580 —South from Reno

U.S. 50 — From the west (Lake Tahoe) or east

U.S. 395 — North from California

U.S. 95 — From Las Vegas, north to U.S. 50, then west

Twain said he'd heard the story from conductors, landlords, passengers, drivers, and others. (The same driver even regaled him with it two or three times in the same afternoon, or so he said.) It had been published so many times, he quipped, that he had heard it was in the Talmud and employed in the Roman inquisition. In the course of six years going back and forth over the Sierra, he said he'd heard it "four-hundred and eighty-one or eighty-two times."

As with any story so often told, it likely changed a bit as time passed. Greeley himself told the story initially, writing about it in his own newspaper, the *Tribune*. But he didn't mention Monk by name. At some point, it was picked up by humorist Artemus Ward, who became both a friend and a role model to Twain, and whose use of the story in his own lectures may have inspired Twain to borrow his mentor's material.

By 1866, when he was starting out on the lecture circuit himself, Twain was using the tale in his own addresses. In fact, he tapped the story in just his second appearance that year. His "colorless, monotonous" delivery (his own description) fell flat with the audience: "There was dead silence," and "the house as a body looked as if it had taken an emetic."

He repeated the story a second time without success the following day before the audience finally warmed to the tale on his third telling.

With all his own telling and retelling — and by committing all this repetition to writing — Twain more than did his part to preserve Monk's legend for the ages. His contention in *Roughing It* that the entire tale was apocryphal came with a wink and a nod to the absurdity of it being told so many times over. Considering Greeley himself didn't even mention Monk in his own account (not to mention that Ward's version placed the journey between

Folsom and Placerville, rather than going east from Nevada), it's hard to know how much of it was true. Monk's brother later confirmed the veracity of the story, or some version of it, stating that the driver had accomplished the feat in a mere four hours.

Regardless, there's no doubt that Monk was highly regarded as a stage driver in his day, earning such nicknames as "King of the Coachmen" and "Knight of the Lash." He was even something of a tourist attraction in his own right. The *San Jose Pioneer* newspaper wrote: "It is said that strangers visiting Carson City would no more think of departing without having seen Hank Monk than a visitor to Rome would omit to take a look at St. Peter's."

Twain wasn't the only author to sing his praises. In her book *The Land of Purple Shadows*, Idah Strobridge calls him "Hank Monk, the incomparable! The most daring — the most reckless of drivers; and the luckiest. The oddest, the drollest of all the most whimsical characters who made Western staging famous the world over."

Famous he was, but not quite as famous as the man who famously tired of hearing his story.

Key Sites in Carson City

Abraham Curry home — 406 N. Nevada St.
First Presbyterian Church — 306 W. Musser St.
Lone Mountain Cemetery — 1044 Beverly Drive
Nevada State Prison (Warm Springs) — 3301 E. 5th St.
Orion Clemens home — 502. N. Division St.
St. Charles Hotel — 310 S. Carson St.
U.S. Mint — 600 N. Carson St.

Como.

Como was one of many mining centers that popped up in the early 1860s east of Carson City.

Como lay on the other side of Dayton in the Pine Nut Mountains, and grew to a population of some 600 people, with a post office, brewery, and telegraph office. The Lyon County town in the Palmyra Mining District quickly outgrew the town of Palmyra itself, and featured

Founded: **1862**
Location: **Lyon County**
Population (1862): **400***
Elevation: **7,116**
Status: **Ghost town**

* Palmyra Mining District

a three-story inn called the Cross Hotel, which had a bar, parlor, meeting hall, and carpeted guest rooms. It was one of four hotels in town, with the *Sonoma County Democrat* lauding another inn, the National, as "a first-class house of refreshments that is second to none this side of the Sierra Slope."

If you didn't like what they served up there, you had your pick of were eight saloons and a brewery. For other services, you could stop at the tin shop, two livery stables, a blacksmith's shop, and one of four dry goods stores.

Top: A horse-powered whim, used for production in small mines, is seen at Como in 1902. **Above:** Como. *William A. Kornmayer Collection; Northeastern Nevada Museum and Historical Society*

Building the new mining town didn't go off without a hitch. Those developing the area had to clear the land by cutting down large numbers of pine trees — the ones that lent their name to the mountain range — which didn't sit well with the Paiutes in the area. The tribe relied on pine nuts harvested from the trees as a food source, so their chief went to the newcomers and protested.

The loggers ignored him, though, and kept right on cutting down trees. Then they got spooked one day when they saw members of the tribe watching them, so they adopted a password to guard against Paiute intruders. They even requested troops from Fort Churchill, who arrived to help them fend off a feared attack. It came, or so they thought, when a pair of miners from Dayton headed toward town and failed to use an agreed-upon password, thereby triggering a barrage of gunfire from the paranoid Como residents.

The ruckus disturbed the Paiutes, whose chief strolled into town to ask what all the fuss was about.

Paiute protests and imaginary incursions aside, Como quickly became a hub of activity, and, in 1864, the site of a steam-driven mill owned by J.D. Winters.

The nascent mining center drew the interest of Alfred Doten, who like Twain and others, spent time as both a journalist and a prospector. When he wasn't prospecting, Doten was doing carpentry work — he built a coffin for a suicide victim out of boards repurposed from a makeshift pigpen. He also wrote for a weekly newspaper in Como called the *Sentinel*, his first gig as a reporter.

Before long, he crossed paths with Twain, who had been sent by the *Enterprise* on a two-week assignment to cover the activity in the new district. Twain, however, had less interest in covering that story than in taking in other sights: specifically, the brewery.

"Mark, you don't seem to get out among the mines and write 'em up," Doten observed on meeting him. "If you'll come along with me to the top of the hill, I'll point you out all the quartz ledges in the district, give you the names of the mines, and the aggravating particulars, just as good as if you draped all around among them yourself. Splendid view, Mark; come along up and I'll give you the whole thing."

In response, Twain smiled and produced a biblical reference: "You remind me of that fellow we read of in the Bible, called the devil, who took the Savior up on top of a high mountain, where he could see all over the world, and offered to give him the whole thing if he would fall down and worship him. Only you ain't the devil and I ain't the Savior by a blamed sight. How far do you say it is up there? Only half a mile? Well, no thank you all the same, but I'm too derned lazy. Let's go down to the brewery."

It wasn't as though Twain tried to hide his laziness — or his attraction to the brewery — even from his readers.

In a report for the *Enterprise*, he stated flatly: "This new mining town, with its romantic name, is one of the best populated and most promising camps, but as to the mines, I have started out several times to inspect them, but never could get past the brewery."

Como's Comedown

Promising or not, Como failed to live up to the hype. By 1864, it was in decline. The Cross Hotel was moved to nearby Dayton and ultimately burned to the ground. The *Sentinel*'s publishers moved to Dayton, too, having pulled the plug on the newspaper in July of 1864 after just 13 issues.

Doten, meanwhile, moved on to write for the *Virginia Daily Union* and *Territorial Enterprise* before serving as editor of the *Gold Hill Daily News*.

Getting to Como

U.S. 50 — From Highway 50, take Dayton Valley Road east to Old Como Road. This road is chunky gravel with some large rocks; slow speed is advised and 4-wheel-drive is preferred.

Dayton.

Dayton and Genoa residents like to debate which of the two towns qualifies as the first continuous settlement in Nevada. Regardless of which side of the fence you come down on, they've both been around a long time.

Founded: **c. 1850**
Location: **Lyon County**
Population (1870): **918***
Elevation: **4,396**
Status: **Unincorporated town**

* 2020 population: 15,153

Dayton began as a mining community called "Gold Cañon" (canyon) around 1850, but was referred to as "China Town" in the 1860 census because a large number of Chinese workers had emigrated there from California to escape racist taxation policies.

The name "Dayton" was adopted in late 1861 to honor surveyor John Day, who would be elected Nevada's surveyor general seven years later.

One of the area's most prominent residents was a man named Adolph Sutro, a former cloth factory owner and cigar salesman who'd found his way to Virginia City in 1860. On the lookout for a new investment, Sutro hit upon the idea of digging a tunnel from

Virginia City down to the Dayton area that would drain water out of the mines and keep them from flooding.

Somewhere along the way, Mark Twain became acquainted with Sutro, whom he accompanied along with six others on an excursion from Virginia City to Dayton in February of 1864.

The Dayton Courthouse was built in 1864. Dayton was the seat of Lyon County until a couple of years after the courthouse burned in 1909. Then, the county seat was transferred to Yerington.

When they arrived, Twain found Dayton had grown since the last time he'd been there: "We found Dayton the same old place but taking up a good deal more room than it did the last time I saw it." Moreover, it was "looking more brisk and lively with its increase of business, and more handsome on account of the beautiful dressed stone buildings with which it is being embellished of late."

Dayton's Odd Fellows Hall was built in 1863, when Twain was in Nevada. It was remodeled three years later after a fire to host performances, and today is known as the Odeon Hall. *Author photo*

The 30-minute journey involved crossing a sturdy span known as Ball Robert's Bridge. There, Twain said, Sutro's dog Carlo — energized by a healthy breakfast — got into a skirmish with "six or seven other dogs he was entirely unacquainted with, had never met before and probably has no desire to meet again."

Twain tried a bit of wordplay on Sutro, remarking that the bridge was "a credit to that bald gentleman" (a play on the name "Ball Robert"). But the joke fell flat, with Twain noting that the Prussian immigrant was "insensible to the more delicate touches of American wit, and the effort was entirely lost on him."

Undeterred, Twain repeated the joke "once or twice without

producing any visible effect, and finally derived what comfort I could by laughing at it myself."

Instead of recognizing the humor, Sutro "being a confirmed businessman, responded in a practical and businesslike way." He took the occasion to speak up in favor of private enterprise, touting private business as being able to build such a project more soundly and economically than the government could have done. In the government's hands, he declared, "it would have cost an extravagant amount of money and been eternally out of repair."

He even contended that private businessmen could have captured Richmond far more quickly than the Union Army had managed it. "They have fooled away two or three years...," he said, "whereas if they had let the job by contract to some sensible businessman, the thing would have been accomplished and forgotten long ago."

Ironically, it took Sutro far longer than three years to complete his tunnel. He hatched the idea to build it in 1865 and received a charter from Congress for it the following year. However, William Ralston of the Bank of California reneged on an offer to finance the project, and it was only after the catastrophic fire of 1869 in the Yellow Jacket Mine that it picked up steam again, supported by miners in the region.

Even then, the nearly four-mile-long tunnel wasn't completed until 1878 and didn't start operating until the following summer, whereupon mine owners rented it for $10,000 a day because it could drain 4 million gallons of water in that time.

Getting to Dayton

U.S. 50 — Dayton is about 13 miles east of Carson City and 50 miles west of Fallon on Highway 50.

The Sutro Tunnel. *Library of Congress*

Sutro promptly sold his interest in the tunnel, and his brother wound up running it. Sutro, for his part, returned to San Francisco, where he was elected mayor in 1894, serving for two years. He died in 1898, but the tunnel continued operating until the 1940s.

Dayton, meanwhile, served as Lyon County seat until 1911, when the seat shifted to Yerington two years after a fire engulfed the courthouse.

Twain would return to Dayton on his 1866 lecture tour, stopping there Nov. 8 of that year.

Key Sites in Dayton

Camel barn — 200 Pike St.

Odeon Hall — 65 Pike St.

Rock Point Mill — Remains north of U.S. 50

Sutro Tunnel — Sutro Tunnel Road (private)

Wells Fargo station ruins, plaque — Main and Pike streets

From top: Remains of the Rock Point Mill at Dayton, the first major quartz mill in Nevada, built in 1860 or 1861; ruins of 1861 Pony Express station; a stone camel barn, built around the same time, sheltered camels that transported wood, salt, and supplies to Gold Hill and Silver City. All three buildings likely existed when Sam Clemens visited Dayton. *Author photos*

Empire City.

You'd be hard-pressed to find Empire City (also known simply as Empire) today. Just east of Carson City on the Carson River, it was the site of the river's first mill and, by the 1870 census, counted more than 600 residents.

The old Empire cemetery is about the only evidence that this once-thriving mill town ever existed.

Before the city sprang up, a stage stop called Dutch Nick's (after proprietor Nicholas Ambrose) operated in the area. Between the stagecoach station and Empire City itself supposedly lay what Mark Twain referred to as a "great pine forest," at the edge of which lay a log house belonging to a man named Philip Hopkins, his wife, and nine children.

Founded: **1860**
Location: **East of Carson City**
Population (1870): **626**
Elevation: **4,620**
Status: **Cemetery remains***

* *Part of Carson City*

Hopkins, 42, had been heavily invested in one of the best mines at Gold Hill. At the advice of a relative, an editor at the *San Francisco Bulletin*, he sold his shares and invested what he'd earned in the Spring Valley Water Company of San Francisco.

It turned out to be a bad move.

The water company had been cooking the books, and his stock was all but worthless.

Apparently despondent over his losses, Hopkins flew into a mad rage. According to a story attributed to Abe Curry of Carson — a reliable source if ever there was one — Hopkins became prone to fits of violence. His wife feared for his sanity, but her concerns were dismissed as exaggerations until one fateful Monday evening in October of 1863.

Anyone who knew the area might have surmised that Hopkins had been drinking too much "tarantula juice," a homemade brew of wood alcohol that included such ingredients as strychnine and tobacco juice. The concoction may have gotten its name from one of its alleged aftereffects: the sensation of spiders crawling all over one's skin.

Dutch Nick's obituary stated that his saloon served "a drink of liquid that, in five minutes after imbibing, would turn a man into a fiend, or else make him think he had the Comstock Lode in his vest-pocket."

Though Twain never mentions "tarantula juice," he does refer to Dutch Nick's. And such a description would certainly have applied to Hopkins, whose supposed good fortune in the Comstock was followed by his transformation into a fiend.

His account continued: That night at about 10 o'clock, Twain reported, "Hopkins dashed into Carson on horseback, with his throat cut from ear to ear, and bearing in his hand a reeking scalp from which the warm, smoking blood was still dripping, and fell in a dying condition in front of the Magnolia saloon. Hopkins expired in the course of five minutes, without speaking. The long red hair of the scalp he bore marked it as that of Mrs. Hopkins."

Nick Ambrose's home is one of the few remaining traces of Empire City, later known simply as Empire. *Author photo*

Sheriff D.J. Gasherie, a former deputy who served from 1862 to 1864, rode out to the Hopkins home and found the body of Mrs. Hopkins lying on the threshold, her head split with an ax and her right hand nearly severed at the wrist. Six of the couple's nine children were found dead in their rooms, having been beaten over the head with a club, and the eldest was found stabbed to death in the attic.

Two other girls managed to survive.

They said their father had gone berserk after they suggested he calm down and retire for the evening.

Twain closed his report of the tragedy with a rebuke of the San Francisco newspapers, which he said had "permitted this [Spring Valley] water company to go on borrowing money and cooking dividends, under cover of which cunning financiers crept out of the tottering concern, leaving the crash to come upon poor and unsuspecting stockholders, without offering to expose the villainy at work. We hope the fearful massacre detailed above may prove the saddest result of their silence."

But it was Twain, not his fellow journalists in San Francisco, who was putting one over on his readers. Anyone who lived in the area would have known there was no "great pine forest" between Dutch Nick's and Empire City — which, in fact, shared the *exact same location*. Besides, the real Phillip Hopkins was a bachelor.

The entire article was a hoax.

The Carson River is seen from the Empire Cemetery. Dutch Nick's saloon was likely somewhere near this spot. *Author photo*

But the furor that followed Twain's fictional account presaged the frenzy that would accompany Orson Welles' famous *War of the Worlds* broadcast in 1938. Other newspapers picked up the sensational story and were chagrined to find out it was all just a satire meant to skewer San Francisco newspapers and utility companies for cooking the books and artificially inflating stock prices. Like any fable, the article ended with "the moral of the story."

Twain immediately printed a retraction titled "I Take it All Back," but newspapers in Sacramento and San Francisco that had run with the story demanded that he resign — which he offered to do before being persuaded by editor Joseph Goodman to stay on the job.

Twain claimed to have been caught entirely off-guard by the response, later writing that "the idea that anybody could ever take my massacre for a genuine occurrence never once suggested itself to me. But I found out then, and never have forgotten since, that we never read the dull explanatory surroundings of marvelously exciting things when we have no occasion to suppose that some irresponsible scribbler is trying to defraud us. We skip all that, and hasten to revel in the blood-curdling particulars and be happy."

Headstones at the Empire Cemetery in 2020. *Author photo*

Empire City before it became a memory.

Getting to Empire City

U.S. 50 — Empire is on the eastern edge of Carson City. Take Empire Ranch Road south to Morgan Mill Road to find Dutch Nick's house, then take Morgan Mill Road east to the old cemetery (a steep uphill climb on foot).

Oddly enough, Twain was reportedly scheduled to deliver a speech on the topic of "The Massacre of the Hopkins Family" in October of 1866.

The venue?

Dutch Nick's.

If the belief in Twain's tall tale was short-lived, the existence of Empire City proved nearly as ephemeral. By 1880, its population was barely half of what it had been a decade earlier, and it no longer appeared on census rolls after 1910. It was, however, the home of two notable Nevada citizens. Anne Henrietta Martin served as the first head of the History Department at the University of Nevada, and was the first woman to run for U.S. Senate, losing in 1918 and again two years later. Edwin Roberts, who served for eight years in Congress and a decade as Reno mayor, was a schoolteacher there before beginning his political career.

Key Sites in Empire City

Dutch Nick's home — Empire Ranch and Morgan Hill roads *(southeast corner)*

Empire Cemetery — Up hill north of Morgan Hill Road

STEPHEN H. PROVOST

Genoa.

Mark Twain once recalled a visit to Walley's Hot Springs in a letter he submitted to a newspaper.

David Walley, who'd traveled west from New York, came across the hot springs while he was digging a tunnel about a mile and a half from the town of Genoa. He purchased the land where he found them and started charging 50 cents to anyone who wanted to use them.

Founded: **1851**
Location: **Douglas County**
Population (1860): **155***
Elevation: **4,806**
Status: **Unincorporated town**

* 2020 population: 1,343

He made a killing.

In fact, by 1862, he and his wife Harriet had enough capital ($100,000) to build a 40-room hotel with a ballroom, 11 bathrooms, stables, and bathhouses. He also employed his own physician and a masseur.

Whatever the hot springs charged Twain for the privilege of indulging in their therapeutic waters was, at least according to him, more than worth it.

"These springs, without a doubt, have no equal on this coast for the cure of rheumatism and all afflictions that necessitate me visiting them," he wrote. "I now leave without crutch or cane, entirely well, not only relieved from pain but gained in spirit."

David Walley died in 1875, and his widow kept operating the hot springs resort until her death in 1896.

Getting to Genoa

U.S. 395 — Coming from the north, take Jacks Valley Road east, then follow it south about 8 miles. From the south, take Nevada Route 206 (Genoa Lane) west from 395 about 4 miles to Genoa. Walley's Hot Springs is about 2 miles south of Genoa on NR 206.

In Genoa, Twain may well have stopped in at the Genoa Bar and Saloon on Main Street. Nevada's oldest watering hole, it was founded in 1853 as Livingston's Exchange, a gentlemen's parlor. *Author photo*

It's not surprising that Twain should have visited Genoa, which is just 13 miles south and slightly west of Carson City at the base of the Sierra Nevada mountains. Mormon settlers established a trading post there in 1851, and it lays claim to being the oldest town in Nevada.

Twain wasn't the only famous person to visit Walley's. Clark Gable and Carole Lombard also did. So did fellow stars Ida Lupino and Ray Bolger, along with presidents U.S. Grant and Teddy Roosevelt. And on October 1, 1934, FBI agents shot Chicago mobster Baby Face Nelson at the hot springs after he hid out in a two-room cottage there before returning to the Windy City.

Key Sites in Genoa

Genoa Bar and Saloon — 2282 Main St.
Walley's Hot Springs — 2001 Foothill Road (NR 206)

Gold Hill.

Gold Hill had its own newspaper, the *Daily News* — which wasn't a particular fan of Mark Twain.

He didn't seem to care much for the rival publication either.

On the heels of Twain's satire on the imaginary massacre at Dutch Nick's, the *Gold Hill Daily News* chastened him by calling the piece a "LIE." (It congratulated itself on showing restraint by printing the word in small caps.)

Founded: **1859**
Location: **Storey County***
Population (1862): **1,297****
Elevation: **4,806**
Status: **Unincorporated town**

* Just south of Virginia City
* 2020 population: 191

But the "thin-skinned young man" — Twain, that is — was not amused and also blasted the *San Francisco Bulletin* for leveling similar criticism against him According to the *Daily News*, the *Bulletin* had sent him a "just, calm, and not abusive rebuke." Twain had responded by calling its editor an "oyster-brained idiot."

The *Daily News* was quick to deny any animosity toward the *Enterprise* as a whole: "Leaving the broad and side-splitting humor of Mark Twain out of the question, the *Enterprise* has our best wishes. As to the patronizing portion of his remarks, we simply 'thank him for nothing.'"

Gold Hill in 1860. *Library of Congress*

Beer, Not Gold

Alf Doten, who later became editor of the *Daily News*, wasn't hostile to Twain at all. In fact, Twain had a friendly rivalry with several journalists in the area, including his colleague Dan De Quille and staffers of the rival *Virginia Daily Union*. (Virginia City was large enough to have four newspapers in 1864, and the *Union* published from 1862 to 1867.)

Doten's extensive journals describe "a pleasant little chat" with Twain upon meeting him in March of 1864.

They soon became friends, fellow prospectors, and drinking

companions.

Twain's thirst for beer, as expressed to Doten, was recalled in a tale told by his son, Professor Samuel B. Doten, to a gathering at the Reno Lions Club in 1947.

According to the younger Doten, Twain was strolling around a canyon near Gold Hill when he saw a chunk of ore lying on the surface of the ground: pure white quartz with specks and a thread of gold running through it. Twain staked a claim, and Doten lent a hand, asking Twain what he was going to call it.

"Inspiration," he answered.

But the inspiration soon wore off as they kept digging through the morning without result, creating a large hole in the mountain as the weather began to warm up. It got so hot that Doten removed his shirt and kept working, naked from the waist up.

"Alf, I think we can change the name of this from 'Inspiration' to 'Perspiration,'" Twain finally remarked. "I have a thirst, and I want beer."

Doten agreed.

How thirsty was Twain?

"Let's go back to Gold Hill and get some beer," he prompted. "I don't want beer by the glass, I want it in horse buckets, all I can drink and more after that."

He didn't say where in Gold Hill they ended up drinking, but they had plenty of options. Sixteen saloons were operating in town as of 1864 with names such as Finch's, White & Youst, and the San Juan Exchange.

The bar at the Gold Hill Hotel was another possibility. The hotel, which still exists today, boasts of being the oldest in the state, having opened in 1859 as the Riesen House. The current building opened as a single-story brick structure two years later, and was purchased by Horace M. Vesey the following year (1862). It then became Vesey's Hotel, tacking on a wooden addition later in the decade.

Right behind the hotel was the infamous Yellow Jacket Mine, where some 35 miners died in a fire on April 7, 1869. But by that time, Twain was no longer in Nevada.

Mark Twain may have stopped in at the Gold Hill Hotel, which was known as Vesey's during his time in Nevada. *Author photo*

Getting to Gold Hill

U.S. 50 — Gold Hill is about 4 miles north of U.S. 50 via Nevada Route 341. The turnoff is just east of Mound House.

The Yellow Jacket Mine is just behind the Gold Hill Hotel.
Author photo

Touring Celebrity

Two years after leaving Nevada (for that story, see the Virginia City section) Twain returned to Gold Hill in 1866 as part of a more than two-month-long tour of California and Nevada that featured some 16 engagements — including six in the Carson-Virginia City area.

The tour, which included stops at Dayton, Silver City, and

Gold Hill, ended on an ignominious note thanks to some friends of Twain's, who discovered that — when it came to having a laugh at someone else's expense — he was a lot better at dishing it out than he was at taking it.

After the stop in Gold Hill, Twain was headed back to Virginia City on foot around 11 at night when five or six armed, masked men ambushed him and demanded that he turn over his valuables. They addressed one another as "Beauregard," "Phil Sheridan," and "Stonewall Jackson."

It wasn't a surprising development, as Twain himself admitted the "divide" — a high, unpopulated space between the two towns — had been "the scene of twenty midnight murders and a hundred robberies."

Make that a hundred-and-one.

The highwaymen had been waiting there for two hours to waylay Twain, who was accompanied by his agent, Denis McCarthy.

After a series of threats to "Throttle him! Gag him! Kill him!" they ultimately made off with his $300 gold watch (a gift received more than two years earlier), two jackknives, three lead pencils, and $125 in cash.

The "cold freezing night," which Twain's friend Alf Doten described as "cloudy, cool & disagreeable," made the whole experience even more disagreeable. Nonetheless, Twain put an ad in the paper the following morning, offering to negotiate payment for the stolen watch.

It turned out to be unnecessary.

As he was leaving on the stage for California, a package containing his belongings was handed to him. It turned out the whole thing had been a prank.

Nevada Lectures

1863

July 8 — Carson House, Virginia City (opening of new hotel)

October — Eagle Fire Company celebration, Virginia City

1864

January 27 — Courthouse, Carson City

1866

October 31 — Maguire's Opera House, Virginia City

November 3 — Carson City

November — Washoe City

November 8 — Dayton, Nevada

November 9 — Silver City

November 10 — Gold Hill Theatre

1868

April 27 — Piper's Opera House, Virginia City

April 28 — Piper's Opera House, Virginia City

April 29 — Carson City

April 30 — Carson City (school benefit)

McCarthy had even been in on it.

"Mark was considerably taken down," Alf Doten later wrote, "but saw through the whole thing at once. He couldn't see the joke much, however, and talked to the boys quite profanely until the stage drove off. ... They were only trying, however, to play even on him for some of his practical jokes of former times."

The *Gold Hill Daily News* called it "a splendid joke, but Mark can't see the point."

The holdup, as depicted in *Roughing It*.

He complained bitterly that the incident had made him sweat, and the "perspiration gave me a cold which developed itself into a troublesome disease and kept my hands idle some three months, besides costing me quite a sum in doctor's bills."

Though it made him physically sick, the prank apparently cured him of something else: his own penchant for practical jokes. "Since then," he wrote several years later, "I play no practical jokes on people and generally lose my temper when one is played on me."

Twain never returned to lecture at Gold Hill or Silver City after that, although he did speak twice more in Virginia City and once in Carson two years later as part of a tour discussing "Pilgrim Life." (He also spoke at a school benefit in Carson City during that trip.) Those 1868 appearances marked the last time Twain visited the state of Nevada.

Gold Hill continued to grow after Twain left Virginia, as seen in these photos from 1867 (top) and 1875. *Library of Congress*

Key Sites in Gold Hill

Gold Hill Hotel (Vesey's) — 1540 S. Main St.

Bank of California — Just north of hotel, west side of road

The Bank of California!

AGENCY, ...GOLD HILL, Nev

WM. SHARON, Gen'l Agent.

THIS AGENCY IS NOW PREPARED TO receive Deposits of COIN or BULLION. either on

OPEN ACCOUNT,

Or to Issue Certificates Therefor!

Payable (at the option of the holder in Gold Hill or in San Francisco; to make Collections; purchase Bullion at the most favorable rates, or advance coin thereon when forwarded to the Parent Bank in San Francisco; sells Bills of Exchange; and transact a General Banking Business.

Checks for Sale on

London.	Paris,
Bank of Ireland (Dublin),	New York,
San Francisco.	Boston,
Portland (Oregon),	Sacramento, etc.

WM. SHARON. General Agent.
W. H. BLAUVELT, Cashier.
Gold Hill, May 1, 1865. jyl tf

Top: The Miners Union Hall, seen in 1940. *Library of Congress*

Above: William Sharon controlled the Bank of California's branch in Gold Hill, which ran the ad at left in the Gold Hill Daily News. *Author photo*

VESEY HOTEL,

MAIN STREET,

(above Blanchard,)

GOLD HILL, NEVADA TERRITORY,

H. M. VESEY,

RIETOR.

VESEY HOTEL

—AND—

RESTAURANT!

Main street, Gold Hill.

JAMES LOWREY,......Proprietor.

THE ABOVE PROPRIETOR, HAVING rented this well known House, has had the Lodging Department thoroughly renovated, and will conduct the Dining Room in Restaurant style.

The tables will always be supplied with the best the market affords.

Meals at all hours. Board by the Meal, Day or Week. The patronage of the public is generally solicited. JAMES LOWREY.

VESEY BAR,

—IN THE—

Vesey Hotel, Gold Hill.

This Bar is furnished with the best

Liquors, Cigars and Tobaccos!

generally solicited.

The public I

Gold Hill, S

Mark Twain may have stopped for a drink at Vesey's Hotel and T.E. Finch's saloon, two of several bars in Gold Hill.

T. E. FINCH'S

SALOON,

Main Street, Gold Hill, N. T.

TOBACCO, CIGARS, CUTLERY,

STATIONERY AND FANCY ARTICLES,

ALWAYS ON HAND.

Dealers in School Books and Cheap Publications.

Gravelly Ford.

There wasn't much at Gravelly Ford on the Humboldt River in the early 1860s. But Sam Clemens did write a story about the place shortly after he started working for the *Territorial Enterprise* in early October of 1862 — not a word of which was true.

The story recounted the discovery of a nearly century-old "stone mummy" in the mountains south of Gravelly Ford. Why did he choose Gravelly Ford as the setting for this tall tale?

Founded: **1860s**
Location: **Eureka County**
Population (1889): **42**
Elevation: **4,734**
Status: **No longer exists**

Maybe because it was so far away from Virginia City that no one could investigate the veracity of his claims by going there.

After all, they should have known they were bogus just from reading the story.

The Eureka County site was noteworthy as a pioneer crossing. The Donner Party had camped there, and in fact, it was said to have been the site of a famous dispute between John Snyder and James F. Reed. The dispute began, as so many do, with an exchange of words, which soon escalated and ultimately led to violence.

Snyder took out a whip and hit Reed hard with the butt end of it. He then cracked the whip at Reed twice more, the first time cutting a deep gash in his face. Upon witnessing this, Reed's wife raced forward and tried to stop the violence by jumping between them, but only succeeded in getting lashed herself.

An enraged Reed pulled out his hunting knife and thrust it into Snyder's breast, puncturing his lung. He died, and the party decided to banish Reed as punishment; he was forced to leave his family behind.

Amazingly, Reed and his family both lived to be reunited. Reed survived and made it to California, while the Donner Party was snowed in at Donner Lake. Reed was in the party that rescued them, and was fortunate enough to find that his family was one of just two in the party to have survived intact.

It was a great story, but it happened 14 years before Clemens' arrival in Carson City, and it was not the one he now told. Neither did he relate a tragic story that had occurred just recently, in 1861. Native Americans massacred a wagon train in the area; a woman from the tribe attempted to save a child in the wagon party, but she was chased for days and ultimately caught. The child was killed.

Clemens' story was fascinating in its own right, though.

He reported that when the "petrified man" was found near Gravelly Ford, "every limb and feature of the stony mummy was perfect, not even excepting the left leg, which has evidently been a wooden one during the lifetime of the owner."

He then went into great detail about the discovery: "The body was in a sitting posture, and leaning against a huge mass of croppings; the attitude was pensive, the right thumb resting against the side of the nose; the left thumb partially supported the chin, the fore-finger pressing the inner corner of the left eye and drawing it partly open; the right eye was closed, and the fingers of the right hand spread apart."

It was, as Clemens would later declare, "a string of roaring absurdities" designed to lampoon so-called discoveries of petrified men that were circulating at the time.

The "petrified man," as depicted in Twain's *Sketches New and Old*.

"One could scarcely pick up a paper without finding in it one or two glorified discoveries of this kind," he later explained. "The mania was becoming a little ridiculous. I was a brand-new local editor in Virginia City, and I felt called upon to destroy this growing evil; we all have our benignant, fatherly moods at one time or another, I suppose. I chose to kill the petrifaction mania with a delicate, a very delicate satire."

The idea of such a satire wasn't exactly original, though. Another spoof had appeared in an 1858 issue of the *Alta California* newspaper. In that article, a fake German medical doctor named Friederich Licthenberger "submitted" a "letter" concerning a prospector named Ernest Flucterspiegel. The man supposedly drank half a pint of some liquid he'd discovered inside a geode, which made him so sick it killed him — and turned him to stone.

The doctor who'd written the letter reported that, during a crude autopsy performed with a hatchet, he'd dissected the body and found that the heart "strongly resembled a piece of red jasper."

Despite the ridiculous nature of these tales, the public was captivated. So rather than discrediting them, as he had intended, Clemens only fueled the fire with his story. Other newspapers reprinted it, and it was so widely disseminated as fact that Clemens was later "stunned to see the creature I had begotten to pull down the wonder-business with, and bring derision upon it, calmly exalted to the grand chief place in the list of the genuine marvels our Nevada had produced."

(Clemens also sought to mock a judge in Humboldt County named Justice Sowell, whom he depicted in the story as holding an inquest to determine the petrified man's cause of death.)

Doubtless to Clemens' chagrin, more such hoaxes appeared. The most famous of them, the so-called Cardiff Giant, was invented in 1868 by an atheist named George Hill. Hill had recently argued against the account in Genesis that giants once roamed the earth. The argument took place at a Christian revival meeting, so Hill (predictably) lost.

He therefore set out to demonstrate how easy it was to dupe people into believing the absurd, creating a 10-foot-tall stone statue and burying it, then exhuming it and showing off his "discovery" in Cardiff, New York. Although some recognized it as a fake, many people were inclined to believe that it was one of the giants mentioned in Genesis. In fact, hundreds of people started coming by every day to see the statue at 50 cents apiece for a 15-minute viewing session.

Hull eventually sold his interest in the giant to a syndicate led by David Hannum for $23,000, and Hannum's group put it on display. P.T. Barnum, the consummate showman and promoter, offered $50,000 for it, but Hannum refused, and Barnum had a replica created that he displayed at his museum in New York.

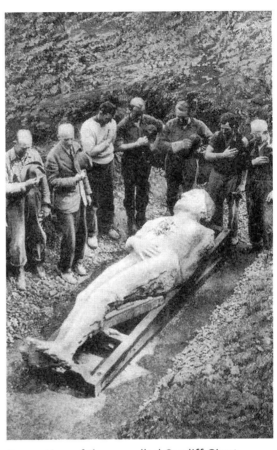

When Hannum heard about it, he was quoted as saying, "There's a sucker born every minute" — a quote later widely (and falsely) attributed to Barnum.

The whole thing was exposed as a hoax in December of 1869, when Hull admitted it was a fraud. The following year, Mark Twain poked fun at

Excavation of the so-called Cardiff Giant, 1869.

the charade in "A Ghost Story" — the ghost being that of the Cardiff Giant. In the tale, the confused spirit wants to be returned to his original burial place, but instead winds up haunting Barnum's museum.

And what of Gravelly Ford? A small town did spring up there sometime in the 1860s, housing workers on the Central Pacific Railroad, and it survived at least until 1889, when it had a telegraph station, restaurant, and store, along with a meager population of 42.

Today, there's nothing left but some depressions in the earth, making it less than a ghost town, but still with more spirit than the imaginary Cardiff Giant's ghost,

Getting to Gravelly Ford

I-80 — From Interstate 80 east of Battle Mountain, turn south on Nevada Route 306 for a short distance, then follow the Humboldt River east.

Lake Tahoe.

The names in Mark Twain's Nevada weren't always the same as they are today — and he didn't always like it when changes were proposed.

Take Lake Tahoe, for example. It wasn't always called Lake Tahoe.

John C. Frémont dubbed it Lake Bonpland in honor of a French botanist, but the name didn't stick, and people instead began calling it simply "Frémont's Lake." John Calhoun Johnson, a Sierra explorer, proposed the name Fallen Leaf Lake in honor of his

Explored: **1844***
Location: **Nevada/California line**
Elevation: **6,225**
Status: **National Forest land, ski resorts, vacation destinations**

* *John C. Frémont expedition*

Native American guide. Then he became a snowshoe-clad mail carrier who traveled between Placerville and Nevada City, at which point he decided to call it Lake Bigler after John Bigler, the third governor of California.

That's what William Eddy, California's surveyor general, called it in 1853.

But part of the lake was in Nevada, so naming it for a California governor must have seemed a bit unfair to Silver Staters. Besides, at the outset of the Civil War, Bigler backed the Confederacy, leading Union supporters to dislike the name.

One suggested name, Tula Tulia, failed to gain traction. Then, in 1862, Henry DeGroot of the *Sacramento Union* suggested Tahoe, a local tribal word he said translated as "Water in a High Place."

Twain didn't like the name, though. Not one bit.

He thought Tahoe meant, in the Paiute tongue, "grasshopper soup, and derided it as "disgustingly sick and silly name" and a "spoony, slobbering, summer-complaint of a name" that sounded "as weak as soup for a sick infant."

"Of course Indian names are more fitting than any others for our beautiful lakes and rivers, which knew their race ages ago, perhaps, in the morning of creation, but let us have none so repulsive to the ear as 'Tahoe' for the beautiful relic of fairy-land forgotten and left asleep in the snowy Sierras when the little elves fled from their ancient haunts and quitted the earth. They say it means 'Fallen Leaf' — well suppose it meant fallen devil or fallen angel, would that render its hideous, discordant syllables more endurable? Not if I know myself."

Twain embarked on this diatribe in the fall of 1863, but by that time, matters had already been decided by Department of the Interior cartographer William Henry Knight.

Knight rendered the verdict for Tahoe simply by using the label on his maps of the region.

And not to Twain's liking.

As Knight explained: "I remarked [to many] that people had expressed dissatisfaction with the name 'Bigler,' bestowed in honor of a man who had not distinguished himself by any single achievement, and I thought now would be a good time to select an appropriate name and fix it forever on that beautiful sheet of water."

Maps issued by the Federal Land Office in 1862 carried the name "Tahoe," but the issue wasn't quite resolved. When a toll road along the lake was completed in 1863, it was called the Lake Bigler Toll Road. In 1870, the California Legislature passed a bill affirming the name "Bigler," and the Golden State stuck to its guns all the way up until 1945, when it formally changed the name to Tahoe.

Finally.

Twain was doubtless rolling over in his grave.

Firebug Sam

Twain's objections to the name "Tahoe" notwithstanding, he hardly failed to appreciate its beauty. In August of 1861, just a couple of weeks after arriving in Carson City, he and a friend named Johnny Kinney decided to see for themselves what they'd heard described as "the marvelous beauty of Lake Tahoe."

Kinney had come from Ohio with a judge named George Turner, who like Orion Clemens had been appointed to a post in the new territorial government: in this case, as chief justice of its supreme court. The younger Clemens and Kinney, lacking such official sanction, needed to find a way to support themselves.

Hence, their adventure was more than just a lark. Rather, they intended to "take up a wood ranch or so and become wealthy." Translation: They set out to make their fortune in the timber trade.

So they strapped some blankets to their shoulders, grabbed an axe, and set out on foot from Carson City.

Big mistake.

"The reader," Twain later advised, "will find it advantageous to go on horseback."

He'd been told it was just 11 miles to the lake, which was a little optimistic. In fact, it's 12 miles from Carson City to the Spooner Summit trailhead (about three miles east of Lake Tahoe) via U.S. Highway 50... and there were no U.S. highways, for pedestrian, horse traffic, or anything else, back then.

Near the entrance to Clear Creek Canyon, east of Carson City. *Author photo*

At the time, it was the Rufus Walton Toll Road which had opened in 1860 along the modern route of Clear Creek Road, replacing an earlier route called Johnson's Cutoff. A trail through Kings Canyon, from the end of modern King Street/Kings Canyon Road to Spooner Summit, wasn't established yet. This was the aforementioned Lake Bigler Toll Road, completed in 1863, that would later become part of the first transcontinental auto route, the Lincoln Highway, in 1913.

Alternatively, Clemens and his friend may have taken a trail through Ash Canyon, which was north of both Kings and Clear Creek canyons and would have deposited them closer to the north shore — where he says they found themselves when they reached the lake.

At the time, Ash Canyon was known as Gregory's Canyon, because a certain Mr. Gregory had built a sawmill there, three miles west of town, in 1859. Three years later, however (and a year after Clemens first visited Tahoe), the Gregory mill had been swept away in a flood — a flood that had, nonetheless, spared a second mill, owned by one Alexander Ash. Hence the name change to Ash Canyon.

It's conceivable that Clemens and Kinney could have followed the trail along Ash Creek and over a high ridge that Clemens hyperbolically labeled "about a thousand miles high." On the other side, they may have hiked down to Marlette Lake and on to Tahoe.

However, the Clear Creek road, at the time, was the most common path taken by stagecoaches south of Lake Tahoe. (The other common stagecoach route, Henness Pass, was too far to the north: east of Reno at Truckee.)

Whatever their exact trajectory, the journey turned out to be more arduous and longer than they'd anticipated. As they proceeded west out of Carson, they kept searching in vain for some sign of the lake:

"We tramped a long time on level ground, and then toiled laboriously up a mountain about a thousand miles high and looked over. No lake there. "We descended on the other side, crossed the valley, and toiled up another mountain, three or four thousand miles high, apparently, and looked again. No lake yet."

They finally consulted with some Chinese settlers (perhaps workers at one of the mills) and persuaded them to curse the men who'd told them how easy it would be to find the lake. After a brief respite, they were on their way again, and traveled two or three hours more before they finally set eyes on Tahoe: "a noble sheet of blue water lifted six thousand three hundred feet above the level of the sea, and walled in by a rim of snow-clad mountain peaks that towered aloft full three thousand feet higher still!"

They found a boat belonging to a group with a timber claim in the area called the Irish Brigade. This group numbered 14 men, though there were actually only five Irishmen among their number. The Brigade was headed by none other than "Captain" John Nye, Clemens' friend and the brother of Governor Nye.

Taking possession of the boat, which had evidently been simply left there, the pair headed toward the Brigade camp about three miles away, with Johnny doing the rowing ("not because I mind exertion myself," Clemens demurred, "but because it makes me sick to ride backwards when I am at work").

At the camp, they helped themselves to a supper of hot bread, fried bacon and black coffee. They weren't too worried about being discovered, as the lake was seemingly deserted. Apart from some workers at a sawmill three miles away, Clemens estimated there weren't 15 other human beings along the full circumference of the lakeshore.

The water level was lower by a good six feet then, as the first dam at Tahoe City wouldn't be built for nearly a decade.

After a good smoke, they enjoyed a sound night's sleep, lulled to slumber by the sound of the water lapping up against the shore and heedless of an ant colony that invaded their clothes and marched across their unmoving bodies. Then, in the morning, they set out to find a suitable piece of property for their future logging venture, settling on a 300-acre site some three miles up the shoreline and nailing "notices" on a tree to stake their claim. They cut down three trees each to prove their point, then built a brush house on the land the following day.

Then they raided the Brigade camp ("borrow is the more accurate word") for as many cooking utensils and provisions as they could carry.

The western shore of Lake Tahoe, looking northward. *Author photo*

Rather than do any more timber-cutting, they spent the ensuing days floating around on the lake and attempting to fish — with hardly any success. Indeed, they caught, on average, less than one fish a week. Many afternoons were frittered away smoking pipes and reading novels, while they entertained themselves after dark by playing cards around a campfire. Never mind that the cards were "so greasy and defaced that only a whole summer's acquaintance with them could enable the student to tell the ace of clubs from the jack of diamonds."

The Tahoe fire as depicted in *Roughing It.*

One evening, however, they were paying less attention to the campfire than they should have, and Clemens left it unattended to retrieve a frying pan from their boat. Somehow, in the meantime, flames from the campfire had managed to escape and catch on a thick layer of pine needles that blanketed the earth, igniting them "as if they were gunpowder."

A shout from Kinney alerted Clemens, who watched helpless as the fire raged out of control, an inferno reflected perfectly in the waters of the lake. Before Clemens knew it, his coffeepot was incinerated and a "blinding tempest of flame" was "galloping all over the premises," climbing up eight-foot-tall dry manzanita bushes and setting off a series of cracks and pops.

Four hours later, the blaze had traveled beyond their field of vision, and the two men were left looking "like lava men, covered as we were with ashes and begrimed with smoke."

The fire ruined whatever plans the pair may have still had for cutting timber in the area. The trees on their claim were scorched and burned, and the provisions they'd "borrowed" from Nye's Brigade were lost as well. So they did what any sensible person in their situation would do: They returned to the Brigade camp, ate up the rest of the provisions they found there, and skedaddled back to Carson.

To their credit, they repaid the Brigade once they got there and received forgiveness for their actions. Captain Nye even suggested that the shoreline between what is now the location of the Thunderbird Lodge and Sand Point to the north be recognized as "Sam Clemens Bay."

"We made many trips to the lake after that, and had many a hair-breadth escape and blood-curdling adventure which will never be recorded in any history," Twain concluded.

Something else that was never recorded: Their claim to the land they had scoped out along the lake. The Brigade boys didn't follow up on their claim, either, and the land eventually was purchased by others.

In an interesting postscript, Butler Ives — whose team also helped settle the question of Aurora's status as a Nevada town — surveyed the area where Clemens supposedly camped at Tahoe in 1864 and said nothing about burned trees. Another survey, done just three weeks after the fire by James Lawson of the General Land Office, didn't note any burned trees, either.

Was the fire just one of Twain's fanciful tales? An excuse, perhaps, to give up on his timber-cutting ambitions and return to Carson City?

Excuse or not, that's exactly what he did.

Getting to Lake Tahoe

U.S. 50 — To reach north and west shores of Lake Tahoe, the areas where Sam Clemens visited in 1861, take Highway 50 west from Carson City to Nevada Route 28, and follow the shoreline north to Incline Village.

Ragtown.

Sam Clemens passed through Ragtown on his way to Carson City in 1861. It doesn't exist today — and barely did then — at the southern edge of the 40-Mile Desert.

One account of the place, from six years earlier, described it as comprising "three huts, formed by poles, covered with rotting canvas full of holes." By the time Clemens arrived, he observed, "it consisted of one log house and is not set down on a map." An Overland Stage station was, however, established there that year, and there was actually a hotel a mile and a half away.

Founded: **1854**
Location: **Churchill County**
Population (1860): **38**
Elevation: **4,012**
Status: **Highway junction**

The place got its name from the laundry that pioneers left to dry on the bushes in the area. Asa Kenyon established a trading post there in 1854, selling supplies and provisions to trappers, but it was best known as the place you could get water after traveling those parched 40 miles. Kenyon was the only truly permanent settler, but there were some 200 residents — emigrants lying in graves, many having died on the desert crossing or shortly afterward from the effects of the hardship.

A flood destroyed Ragtown and washed away those graves in 1862, a year after Clemens stopped there. But at the time of his arrival, Ragtown must have seemed like an oasis, marking the end of a torturous ride through an unforgiving wasteland. Clemens described it as "forty memorable miles of bottomless sand, into which the coach wheels sunk from six inches to a foot."

He and his companions were forced to get out and walk, which only made things worse, as did the fact that they had no water.

The 40-Mile Desert is just as desolate today as it was in Clemens' time. *Author photo*

"From one extremity of this desert to the other, the road was white with the bones of oxen and horses. It would hardly be an exaggeration to say that we could have walked the forty miles and set our feet on a bone at every step! The desert was one prodigious graveyard," he wrote.

"And the log-chains, wagon tyres, and rotting wrecks of vehicles were almost as thick as the bones. I think we saw log-chains enough rusting there in the desert, to reach across any

State in the Union. Do not these relics suggest something of an idea of the fearful suffering and privation the early emigrants to California endured?"

It was where the Carson River went to die in what Clemens referred to as simply "The 'Sink' of the Carson, a shallow, melancholy sheet of water some eighty or a hundred miles in circumference. Carson River empties into it and is lost — sinks mysteriously into the earth and never appears in the light of the sun again — for the lake has no outlet whatever."

Clemens and his fellow travelers managed to survive the crossing. So did a "poor wanderer" who had lain down to die 10 miles on from Ragtown. "He had walked as long as he could, but his limbs had failed him at last. Hunger and fatigue had conquered him."

Historical marker at the site once occupied by Ragtown, west of Fallon on U.S. 50. *Author photo*

The Clemens party took him aboard their coach and paid his fare to Carson, and he slowly recovered on the way, offering his thanks.

A post office operated at Ragtown from 1864 to 1867, and the place was renamed Leeteville, with a new post office, that was open from 1895 to 1907. It was named for farmer James Leete, but the "ville" suffix was a misnomer. Leete's wife Esther served as the first postmistress, and although a townsite was mapped out in 1921, it was never developed.

Today, Leeteville Junction marks the place where U.S. Highway 50 and U.S. 50 Alternate diverge. A monument nearby marks Ragtown Crossing, "dedicated to those pioneers whose determination brought them across the Forty Mile Desert to this spot and sweet water."

Getting to Ragtown

U.S. 50 — The Ragtown historical marker is about 9 miles west of Fallon at the junction of U.S. 50 and U.S. 50 Alternate.

Silver City.

Silver City, a settlement just south of Gold Hill, had grown up out of the Ophir Mine camp. Sam Clemens doesn't mention it much in his writings, but a passing reference does appear in the first letter he signed as "Mark Twain," addressed to the *Territorial Enterprise* on January 31, 1863, from Carson City.

Founded: **1859**
Location: **Lyon County**
Population (1861): **1,200***
Elevation: **5,066**
Status: **Semi-ghost town**

*2000 population: 170

Traveling to Carson with his boss, *Enterprise* editor Joe Goodman, he wrote:

"I had a cheerful trip down to Carson, in company with that incessant talker, Joseph T. Goodman. I never saw him flooded with such a flow of spirits before. He restrained his conversation, though, until we had traveled three or four miles, and were just crossing the divide between Silver City and Spring Valley..."

Twain's fellow journalist and staff member at the *Territorial Enterprise*, Dan De Quille, lived in Silver City for a time and wrote of the optimism that pervaded the camp in a December 1860 piece for *The Golden Era*:

"It is surprising, even to one who has been constantly on the spot, to observe the vast change which has taken place in a short period of time in the vicinity of Silver City. I took my 4th of July dinner under drooping branches of a willow in the S. Fork of Gold Canyon with not a single house in sight; now my willow tree is gone; there are quartz mills near the spot, and a long street of adobe, frame and stone houses on either side of the ravine, where whole droves of musical jackasses were wont to graze and frolic not 'lang syne.'

"Hotels, saloons, stores and dwellings are constantly being erected, and though we are not given to boast we cannot help feeling that Silver City is going to be *the* place."

C. B. HALL.   L. D. NOYES.

ARCADE SALOON,

OPPOSITE SILVER HOUSE,

MAIN STREET, SILVER CITY.

ALWAYS ON HAND, THE CHOICEST OF

WINES, LIQUORS AND CIGARS.

HALL & NOYES,   -   -   PROPRIETORS.

Silver City didn't grow as large as Gold Hill immediately to the north or Virginia City just beyond, but the 1864 mercantile guide boasted that "some of the finest mills in the Territory, as well as the richest lodes, lay encompassed within her limits."

Several blocks of granite buildings had been erected, and the residential section was pleasing to the eye, according to the guide.

"Almost every private residence is adorned by numerous trees planted around their dwellings, which has the effect of making favorable impressions on every one that either passes through or takes up a residence within its limits. Silver City is fully represented by societies, organizations and social institutions, which for numbers and unity, would be creditable to the reputation of larger cities."

A new toll road between Silver City and American City was nearly complete, and some 15 mills were operating. Seven hotels were open in the city — up from four in 1861 — along with 10 saloons and half a dozen grocers. It was also home to the first iron works in Nevada.

A newspaper, the *Lyon County Sentinel*, was produced there from 1864 to 1866.

Silver City before 1900.

Getting to Silver City

U.S. 50 — Silver City is about 3 miles north of U.S. 50 via Nevada Route 341. The turnoff is just east of Mound House.

Silver City is a semi-ghost town today, but you can still see old mines and mill works on the hillsides. The Hardwicke House, a former icehouse built in 1862 that later served as a bed and breakfast, is among the historic buildings from Twain's time that are still standing.

The town had likely reached its peak by the time Twain returned for a lecture on the Sandwich Islands (aka Hawaii) on November 9, 1866 as part of his 16-city tour.

Hardwicke House, a former icehouse built in 1862. *Author photo*

Star City.

Its name makes it sound glamorous, like Hollywood, and in its heyday, it was certainly portrayed as a happening place for miners in search of precious ore.

Just a few miles north of Unionville, Star City was home to the storied Queen of Sheba Mine, which produced some $5 million in precious metal between its discovery in 1862 and 1868. That was enough to attract a small army of fortune-seekers to the canyon where silver was first discovered in 1861 and a post office was established the following year.

Founded: **1861**
Location: **Humboldt County***
Population (1863): **1,200****
Elevation: **5,981**
Status: **Ghost town**

* *Now in Pershing County*
** *Just 78 remained by 1871*

By 1863, the city boasted 1,200 residents, a Wells Fargo branch, telegraph office, mercantiles, saloons, and a couple of hotels. The Sheba Mining Company opened a 10-stamp mill to process the ore that worked around the clock.

News of the Sheba mine reached Sam Clemens in Virginia City, and he was duly impressed by the reports. He remarked that Gold Hill, next door to Virginia City, had been the most successful silver-mining site in Nevada to that point. It was, at the height of that success, producing "very rich" ore that yielded $100 to $400 a ton.

The normal yield, however, was much less: $20 to $40 a ton, or a dollar or two for every 100 pounds of ore mined.

There aren't any human residents of Star City these days, but pronghorns, the fastest animals in North America, live nearby. *Author photo*

Star City's silver put those numbers to shame.

Clemens quoted an account from the newspaper that would later employ him, the *Territorial Enterprise*, as saying an assay from the Sheba Mine had placed the value of the yield there at more than $4,000 a ton. Clemens concluded that "the reader will perceive by the above extract, that in Humboldt from one-fourth to nearly half the mass was silver."

Clemens didn't need any more encouragement. He and three companions decided straightaway to head for Humboldt, fearing they'd be late to the game and all the good mines would be secured by the time they got there.

Not surprisingly, almost all the fortune-seekers were men, which created a desire for female companionship that was second only to the prospectors' lust for silver. Such was their state of loneliness that, at one point, Clemens found himself in a "sort of long, post-office single file of miners" at Star City "to patiently await my chance to peep through a crack in the cabin and get a sight of that splendid new sensation — a genuine live Woman!

"At the end of an hour my turn came, and I put my eye to the crack, and there she was, with one arm akimbo, and tossing flap-jacks in a frying-pan with the other. And she was one hundred and sixty-five years old, and hadn't a tooth in her head." He later added, by way of correction, "Being in calmer mood, now, I voluntarily knock off a hundred [years] from that."

Getting to Star City

I-80 — Take Nevada Route 400 south from Interstate 80 at Mill City (27 miles west of Winnemucca). Then go 9.5 miles south to the Star City Historical Marker. The road to that point is well-paved asphalt.

Steamboat Springs.

The natural hot springs at Steamboat Springs have been welcoming vacationers and the infirm for more than 150 years. Native Americans cooked pine nuts over the springs, and settlers used them to cook oxen before they began attracting countless miners and other residents to the Washoe Valley.

Developed: **1859**
Location: **Washoe County**
Population (1860): **196***
Elevation: **4,642**
Status: **Hot springs business**

* Steamboat Valley

The well at the springs earned the name "Chicken Soup," because that was what the water there tasted like.

James Cameron discovered the springs in 1859 and staked a claim there, but it was jumped in 1861 by an Austrian physician named Dr. Ellis, who built a 34-bed hospital and seven bath houses to treat patients using the hot springs' natural healing properties. Within two years, a hotel was operating there under the care of Amos W. Stowe. In addition to lodging and food prepared by his wife, Stowe staged daily shooting matches.

The springs entertained visitors with a 60-foot geyser, and

offered them a "hot time" in sheds constructed over cracks in the earth to create saunas. John Bigler, the California governor for whom Lake Tahoe was once named, visited the springs to "sweat awhile" in 1864, and Ulysses S. Grant later visited the site as well.

A vintage postcard shows geysers at Steamboat Springs in the 1920s.

Mark Twain stayed at the Steamboat Springs Hotel in August of 1863 and wrote a letter about the experience, which as published in the *Territorial Enterprise*.

The springs, he wrote, were natural: "The devil boils the water, and the white steam puffs up out of crevices in the earth, along the summits of a series of low mounds extending in an irregular semi-circle for more than a mile.

"The water is impregnated with a dozen different minerals, each one of which smells viler than its fellow, and the sides of the springs are embellished with very pretty parti-colored incrustations deposited by the water.

"From one spring the boiling water is ejected a foot or more

This ad for the Steamboat Springs hotel appeared in 1865 in the *Gold Hill Daily News.*

by the infernal force at work below, and in the vicinity of all of them one can hear a constant rumbling and surging, somewhat resembling the noises peculiar to a steamboat in motion — hence the name.

Twain would have known, and he must have felt right at home there.

The Steamboat Springs Hotel was " very pleasantly situated on a grassy flat, a stone's throw from the hospital and the bath houses." He praised Stowe, whose table was "furnished with fresh vegetables and meats from numerous fine ranches in the [Washoe] valley."

The springs themselves were recommended for the successful treatment of all diseases except tuberculosis, and a new bath house was being built to accommodate as many as 12 people at a time.

Dr. Ellis had devised a concoction popularly known as a "wake-up-Jake," the news of which awakened Twain's natural sense of curiosity as a reporter. He therefore demanded a dose of the "nauseous mess," which ultimately made him vomit, gave him a nosebleed, and left him "as weak as an infant."

Despite (or perhaps because of) the extreme discomfort

caused by the experience, Twain was convinced of its efficacy. Once he regained his strength, he claimed to be "animated by a higher degree of vigor than I have felt in many a day."

He nonetheless decided against a second or third dose, saying he would sooner have a locomotive travel through him.

"I am about as thoroughly waked up as I care to be."

The Steamboat Springs Resort as it appears in 2022. *Author photo*

Gold in the Goo?

But the springs and their medicinal benefits weren't the only attractions. On the other side lay deposits of tarry black goo that was rumored to be full of gold and silver. That was enough motivation for some opportunists, who apparently sought to take the springs by force.

In February of the following year, the *Gold Hill Daily News* reported that three men had been shot in a property dispute there. Eight men arrived, bent on trouble, but Stowe was expecting the attack and barricaded himself and his employees, all armed with shotguns, inside the building. The attackers were repulsed by gunfire, and three among their party were shot, while no one inside the hotel was hurt.

The trouble wasn't over, though: The same newspaper reported that another attack was expected and that guards were being stationed at the hotel nightly. "It is feared," the report concluded, "that an attempt will be made to burn the hotel and barns."

The hotel had, in fact, burned the previous year and been rebuilt, but no follow-up report was available on this particular threat.

By August of 1865, however, Stowe still ran the hotel and had entirely refitted it to offer a shower, "plunge," or steam experience depending on the visitor's preference.

"Altogether, Steamboat is an excellent resort," the *Daily News* enthused, "and we trust that Stowe will have more guests than he can 'stow' away, who will 'be-stow' upon 'A-mos' a liberal patronage." (The reader was then conveniently referred to an ad for the establishment on the previous page — and continued to run in the publication for the next several weeks.)

In 1867, the buildings on the site, including the improvements made by Ellis, burned down again. At some point, ownership passed to one C.W. Cullins, who purchased the title from original claimant Cameron and cut ties with Dr. Ellis.

Cameron put up a depot for the Virginia & Truckee Railroad, which arrived in the fall of 1871, leading to the development of a small town. But Cullins came to an unfortunate end: He fell into the hot springs while constructing a new bathhouse and died seven days later from the effects of being boiled alive. His widow sold the springs the following year, and the new owners built another hotel.

A post office was established at Steamboat Springs in 1880, but in 1900, an earthquake shifted the ground, causing the hot springs to dry up and capping the geyser. A year later, the Grand Hotel burned to the ground. New wells were drilled after World War I, and the hot springs are still an attraction a century later — minus Dr. Ellis' "wake-up-jake."

Getting to Steamboat Springs

I-580 — Steamboat Springs is west of Interstate 580 between Reno and Carson City. From 580, take Nevada Route 431 east to NR 341, then go south to Steamboat Springs at 16010 S. Virginia St. Road is well-paved asphalt.

Unionville.

Unionville was a town in search of an identity filled with fortune-hunters in search of silver and gold.

Sam Clemens arrived one cold, snowy December in 1861 in a party of four would-be prospectors after a piece in the *Territorial Enterprise* had identified it as the next big thing. There was a buzz about Aurora and the Esmeralda District, to be sure, but it was nothing compared to Unionville.

Founded: **1861**
Location: **Humboldt County***
Population (1863): **1,000**
Elevation: **5,050**
Status: **Near-ghost town**

*** Now in Pershing County**

Once again, Clemens caught gold fever.

"This was enough," he wrote decisively, referring to what he'd read in the article. "The instant we finished reading the... article, four of us decided to go to Humboldt [County]. And we also commenced upbraiding ourselves for not deciding sooner — for we were in terror lest all the rich mines would be found and secured before we got there."

In addition to Clemens, the party consisted of a 60-year-old blacksmith named Mr. Ballou, whose expertise and cautious outlook would be essential; New York lawyer William Clagett (later a member of the U.S. House of Representatives); and another lawyer identified in *Roughing It* as "Oliphant" and in Twain's 1869 book *The Innocents Abroad* as Judge A.W. Oliver.

The trip to Humboldt took 13 days, with two additional days of rest for the horses. Oliver and Clemens gathered sagebrush to build a fire each night, while Ballou — otherwise known as Cornbury S. Tillou — did the cooking. The four slept together under a blanket on the frozen ground, along with a hound dog they'd taken along on the trip that Oliver invited to join them for extra warmth. But he took to pawing Ballou in the back and was duly expelled.

They finally reached the Humboldt River, which Clemens described as "a sickly rivulet."

"One of the pleasantest and most invigorating exercises one can contrive is to run and jump across the Humboldt river till he is overheated, and then drink it dry."

Then it was on to Unionville, where they arrived in the middle of a driving snowstorm. The confusion over its identity lay in the fact that it had recently changed its name: Originally, most of the prospectors who arrived there were Confederate sympathizers, who christened it Dixie. But when more Union backers arrived, the name was changed to Unionville on July 4, 1861, five months before Clemens and company arrived.

Although established as the capital of Humboldt County, there wasn't much to Unionville at the time. By Clemens' account, it consisted of "eleven cabins and a liberty-pole. Six of the cabins were strung along one side of a deep canyon, and the other five faced them."

Clemens' group added to that number by building "a small, rude cabin in the side of the crevice" that they roofed with canvass, leaving one corner of it open to create a chimney.

"The rest of the landscape," he wrote, "was made up of bleak mountain walls that rose so high into the sky from both sides of the canyon that the village was left, as it were, far down in the bottom of a crevice. It was always daylight on the mountain tops a long time before the darkness lifted and revealed Unionville."

Top: The Wells Fargo office in Unionville.
Above: Brick and stone ruins in 2022. *Author photo*

William "Billy" Clagett, left, with Clemens, center, and A.J. Simmons.

All That Glitters...

The party's tent-cabin wasn't particularly sturdy.

It was constructed, Clemens explained, by digging a square in the steep base of the mountain, then setting up a pair of uprights and topping them with two joists.

"Then you stretch a great sheet of 'cotton domestic' from the point where the joists join the hill-side down over the joists to the ground; this makes the roof and the front of the mansion; the sides and back are the dirt walls your digging has left. A chimney is easily made by turning up one corner of the roof."

Having the roof against a hillside proved to be hazardous when an animal happened down the mountain. Once, when Oliver was composing poetry, a mule fell down the chimney, sending fire everywhere and knocking the judge over backward.

This happened a second time about a week and a half later, again while Oliver was composing poetry, with this mule kicking over a candle and wrecking most of the kitchen furniture. It was enough to convince Oliver that he should move to the other side of the canyon (where there were fewer mules). But alas, trouble followed him in the form of a cow.

"One night about eight o'clock he was endeavoring to finish his poem... a stone rolled in — then a hoof appeared below the canvas — then part of a cow — the after part." Dust began streaming down, and before Oliver could get well away, "the entire cow crashed through on to the table and made a shapeless wreck of every thing!"

At that point, Oliver, who Clemens said to this point had "never complained" in his life, finally did so:

"This thing is growing monotonous."

Left: The cabin said to have been occupied by Sam Clemens and his party in Unionville. *Author photo*

Below: Illustration of the cabin from *Roughing It.*

Unionville was still fairly small at this point, and the canyon is fairly narrow, so Oliver probably didn't move too far away.

The small size of the camp was, in a way, good news, because the four of them had beaten most of the rush and, in consequence, would have their choice of potential claims — if they acted quickly.

Clemens, later confessed "without shame" that he "expected to find masses of silver lying all about the ground." And he lost no time in trying to find it, setting out secretly in search of it so as to beat his companions to the riches. When he found what he was sure was a fragment containing gold, he pocketed it, marked the spot where he'd found it, and hurried back to camp.

But despite all his care in sneaking off alone, he wasn't very good at keeping a secret once the supposed riches were in hand.

Upon returning to camp, he started by asking Ballou, the expert, his opinion of their prospects. Ballou pronounced the site to be "fair enough... but overrated." The Sheba mine in nearby Star City "may be rich enough," he said, " but we don't own it; and besides, the rock is so full of base metals that all the science in the world can't work it. We'll not starve, here, but we'll not get rich, I'm afraid."

When the others began talking about going back the way they'd come, Clemens could no longer contain himself.

"Suppose — merely a supposition, of course — suppose you were to find a ledge that would yield two thousand dollars a ton — would that satisfy you?"

Ballou pronounced anyone who might think such things "crazy as a loon," which of course forced Clemens' hand: Now, to support his own assertions, he had to produce the specimen he'd brought back with him.

When he did, however, he was disappointed. Ballou immediately dismissed the rock as "nothing but a lot of granite rubbish and nasty glittering mica that isn't worth ten cents."

Clemens' hopes were deflated but waxed philosophical, quoting Shakespeare to declare that "all that glitters is not gold."

Ballou scoffed that he could go further and say that *nothing* that glitters is gold.

"A Miner's Dream," illustration from *Roughing It.*

From top: Wrecked cabin; disturbed gravesite and broken tombstone at the Unionville Cemetery. *Author photos.*

Nothing But Rocks

Despite the letdown of Clemens' false alarm, the party stuck around, climbing up mountainsides and over rocks, through sagebrush and snow, but finding no silver, let alone gold.

Finally, one day, they climbed up to a mountain ledge where Ballou broke off some fragments with a hammer. Those fragments were quartz, and they contained not only a thin thread of silver but a few flecks of gold as well.

Full of enthusiasm, they posted a notice staking their claim and proudly dubbing the site "Monarch of the Mountains." But it wasn't long before reality settled in: If they wanted to obtain the silver, they'd have to extract it. And that meant a lot of digging, deep into the mountain. The deeper they went, the richer the deposits were likely to be.

After a week of digging with picks and shovels, then blasting the earth with powder when the earth got too hard to dig, they got only 12 feet down and gave up. Then they tried to tunnel into the side of the mountain instead, but they quit again after another week and gave up on the site.

Deciding that staking a claim was easier than digging, they went around nailing up notices, then trading portions of those sites for parts of other miners' claims. In the meantime, more men were streaming into town with gold-laden dreams of their own.

"Prospecting parties swarmed out of town with the first flush of dawn, and swarmed in again at nightfall laden with spoil — rocks. Nothing but rocks," Clemens said. Every man's pockets were full of them; the floor of his cabin was littered with them; they were disposed in labeled rows on his shelves."

Clemens eventually realized that the stories of mountains filled with gold and silver that had lured him there had been exaggerated, to put it mildly. Seeking to bolster their own near-worthless claims and trade them for something better, miners would get the best part of their find assayed. Then they'd act as though it were consistent throughout the entire claim.

"The custom was to hunt out the richest piece of rock and get it assayed!" he explained. "Very often, that piece, the size of a filbert, was the only fragment in a ton that had a particle of metal in it — and yet the assay made it pretend to represent the average value of the ton of rubbish it came from!"

Newspaper reports had bought into these wildly inflated claims, and the rest was history.

The party soon packed up their bags and departed.

Others, however, kept coming to Unionville. By 1863, nearly 1,000 people lived there in a city of 10 stores, nine saloons, and six hotels. By May of that year, it had its own newspaper, the *Humboldt Register*, and the population at one point surged as high as 1,500. But the finds started getting fewer and miners' patience wearing thin after 1864, and a fire in the summer of 1872 — a week after plans for a new Catholic church had been announced — caused $15,000 to $30,000 worth of damage.

The fire started in a drugstore, then spread to a shoe store, a lawyer's office, and the building that housed the Wells Fargo and County Treasurer's offices. It then burned the roof off the County Recorder's and Sheriff's offices.

When the county seat was moved to Winnemucca the following year, it marked the end of Unionville's heyday. It continues to exist today, with the ruins of some old stone buildings and miners' shacks among the vestiges of its time as a boomtown. One of those shacks is purported to be where Twain and his party stayed, though it looks far more permanent than the canvas-covered lean-to described in *Roughing It*.

Getting to Unionville

I-80 — Take Nevada Route 400 south from Interstate 80 at Mill City (27 miles west of Winnemucca). Continue south past the Star City Historical Marker and turn west on Unionville Road, then travel about 3 miles on an easy gravel road.

Ruined stone structure at Unionville. *Author photo*

Virginia City.

Virginia City today looks very much like an Old West town, and many of the buildings there do date back to the 19th century. But that doesn't mean it's the same city it was when Mark Twain worked there at the *Territorial Enterprise*.

The newspaper's original offices in a small wooden building on A Street were replaced the year he left by a fancy new building that still stands on C Street. It's one of the few buildings from that era that has survived.

Founded: **1859**
Location: **Storey County**
Population (1863): **15,000**
Elevation: **6,150**
Status: **County seat**

* 2020 population: 787

Indeed, Most of the city that Twain knew was destroyed in the Great Fire of 1875, which started October 26 in a boarding house on A Street and raged for hours, burning three-quarters of the city. Tailor shops, meat markets, lumber yards, hotels, blacksmith shops... the list went on and on.

Places frequented by Twain like Maguire's Opera House and Piper's Corner Bar went up in flames. Other saloons he may have visited like the Assembly, Delta, Magnolia, Gobey & Williams, and the Washington were all lost. Even brick buildings weren't able to withstand the heat. The famed International Hotel was destroyed and had to be rebuilt. (Its replacement eventually burned down as well, and a mural now marks where it once stood on C Street.)

Lost in the Great Fire

A partial list of buildings lost in the Great Fire of 1875:

Assembly Saloon
Bank of California
Banner Bros. Clothing
Barnett's Clothing
Berk's dry goods
Block & Co. dry goods
Carson Brewery
Central Market
City Hall
Cohn & Isaacs Clothing
Delleplane's Restaurant
Delta Saloon
Dickman's Grocery
Fletcher & Co. Furniture
Gobey & Williams Saloon
Harris Bros. Cigar Shop
Hatch Bros. dry goods
International Hotel

James Kelly Liquor
J.C. Smith Blacksmith Shop
J.J. Cooper Stables
John Gillig's Hardware
M.M. Fredrick's Jewelry
Magnolia Saloon
Mallon's Store
Masel Meat Market
Masonic Block
McMillan & Adams dry goods
Palace Saloon
Philadelphia Brewery
Roos Bros. Clothing
St. Mary's Catholic Church
St. Paul's Episcopal Church
Thiele's Drugstore
Wiegand Assay Office
Wolf's Tailor Shop

Even churches burned.

The fire caused an estimated $7 million in damage at a time when that was a huge amount of money, dealing a savage blow to the driving force of the city's economy: mining. The Consolidated Virginia mill, the Ophir Works, and California Stamp mill were destroyed. So were the passenger and freight depots of the Virginia & Truckee Railroad.

A few places Twain may have visited — such as the 1859 Tahoe House and 1862 Douglas Building — survived. But even though the Douglas Building is emblazoned with the words "The Washoe Club," it wasn't called that in Twain's day. The Washoe Club was a social and business club that met on A Street until the building where its members gathered was destroyed in the fire along with so many others.

The club started meeting in the Douglas Building on C Street after that, but Twain wasn't a member of the 150-member "Millionaire's Club" that frequented the place. He was gone by then. And as local historian Joe Curtis points out, there were only a handful of millionaires in the city back then... and certainly not 150. When he was there, Twain couldn't even afford the more modest fee charged to join: around $200.

Rapid Growth

Even before the fire, Virginia City changed a lot during the time Twain was there, evolving from a town dominated by miners' cabins into a full-fledged metropolitan city. It was already the biggest city in Nevada Territory by the time he arrived, and it grew by leaps and bounds during his time there.

When Adolph Sutro visited in 1860, he described it as "half a dozen stone houses built last fall, some twenty-five wooden houses, and several hundred tents."

That was it.

But 4,000 people were living there by 1862, and a year later, the population had nearly quadrupled, shooting up to an astonishing 15,000.

From top: Author photos of the Douglas Building and Tahoe House, and Grafton Brown's drawing of the Tahoe House as it appeared in the 1860s.

Illustrations by Grafton T. Brown in 1861 show Virginia City as a modest city made up largely of miner's cabins and one-story wood buildings, such as the John Piper Old Corner Bar frequented by Sam Clemens, left, and the Virginia Saloon. *Library of Congress*

"The 'city' of Virginia roosted royally midway up the steep side of Mount Davidson, seven thousand two hundred feet above the level of the sea, and in the clear Nevada atmosphere was visible from a distance of fifty miles!" Twain would recall.

"It claimed a population of fifteen thousand to eighteen thousand, and all day long half of this little army swarmed the streets like bees and the other half swarmed among the drifts and tunnels of the 'Comstock,' hundreds of feet down in the earth directly under those same streets."

Grafton Brown's drawing of the 1861 International Hotel, right, contrasts with the later six-story International that was the tallest in the state, above.

The Territorial Enterprise, originally published in the modest wooden building on A Street shown at right in Grafton Brown's illustration. By 1864, it was operating out of the building seen at top in the author's photo.

C Street sometime prior to the 1875 fire. *Joe Curtis collection*

By 1864, the city boasted 15 hotels, the same number of restaurants, and more than 50 saloons. Eight stage and express companies were operating in town, nearly two dozen doctors had set up practices, and if they couldn't do the job, there were a couple of undertakers.

Illustrated maps created by Grafton T. Brown in 1861 and 1864 show the town's rapid evolution from one of largely wooden structures to a metropolis of two- and three-story stone and brick buildings.

Charles Collins' 1864 mercantile guide and city directory noted "a marked difference in the style and finish of a large proportion of the residences that are being erected. Luxuries and the comforts of a permanent home are being observed in their construction."

The corner of C and Taylor streets was a hub of activity. Grocer Louis Feusier and hardware merchants Gillig and Mott shared a four-story block of brick buildings there. On that same corner, merchants Howell, Black & Bro. had built "a magnificent brick building with a stone basement running clear through from C to D streets."

Another hardware store, McLaughlin & Root, had constructed a four-story building with fronts on both C and D.

Twain's own *Territorial Enterprise* had a fancy new home on C Street described by Collins' directory as "another of the noticeable features of the city," having graduated from a modest wooden building on A Street. It was one of four newspapers in town, along with the *Union*, *Old Paiute*, and *Nevada Pioneer*.

Virginia City in 1866. *Library of Congress*

Twain would recall the labor involved in navigating the streets of this town, built as it was on the side of a mountain.

"The mountain side was so steep that the entire town had a slant to it like a roof," he wrote. "Each street was a terrace, and from each to the next street below the descent was forty or fifty feet. The fronts of the houses were level with the street they faced, but their rear first floors were propped on lofty stilts; a man could stand at a rear first floor window of a C street house and look down the chimneys of the row of houses below him facing D street.

"It was a laborious climb, in that thin atmosphere, to ascend from D to A street, and you were panting and out of breath when you got there."

New churches were being built, too. St. Mary's in the Mountain, built in 1863 for $20,000, could seat 600 Roman Catholic parishioners in a building 100 feet long. (It would outgrow even this substantial building by 1870, when a new church would be erected across the street.) St. Paul's Episcopal at Taylor and F Street had opened earlier in 1863, with room for 250 worshippers. Sadly, both St. Mary's and St. Paul's would be forced to rebuild after being destroyed in the in the Great Fire of '75; both of those structures survive to this day.

Big Bonanza

Mine owners and bankers were the power players in 1860s Virginia City. They were the people with the money, and their driving ambition was to make more of it — no matter how much they had in the first place.

The rush to Virginia City was jump-started in 1859, when Alva Gould discovered the Gould & Curry Mine. (He partnered with Carson City founding father Abraham Curry in the venture.) But both men sold their interests in the mine that same year, and it was left to others to capitalize — literally — on their find.

The Gould & Curry offices built by George Hearst are today popularly known as "Mackay Mansion." *Author photo*

The first superintendent of the Gould & Curry Mining Company bore a familiar name: George Hearst, the father of newspaper tycoon William Randolph Hearst. He was succeeded by "Bonanza King" John Mackay, whose longtime presence in the Gould & Curry offices ultimately earned them the nickname "Mackay Mansion."

Mackay, who had begun to build his fortune as a shareholder in the Kentuck Mine and superintendent of the Bullion Mine, would become the richest miner on the planet and one of four Irishmen known as "Silver Kings" of the Comstock. He and fellow

Irish immigrant James G. Fair, superintendent of the Ophir mine, joined forces and, shortly afterward, added San Francisco stockbrokers Bill O'Brien and Jim Flood to their partnership. This bloc formed one power center in Virginia City.

John Mackay was superintendent of the Bullion Mine. *Library of Congress*

The other was led by William Ralston, founder and president of the Bank of California in San Francisco, and his agent in the Comstock, William Sharon. (You can still see a sign for the now-closed Sharon House restaurant on Taylor Street just off C Street. It occupied the former Bank of California Building. The 1864 vault is still inside what's now the Ponderosa Saloon.)

Sharon exploited Comstock miners' optimism to loan them money, then foreclosed on their mines when they hit a dry spell. While other lenders were charging 3 to 5 percent interest, Sharon undercut them with a 2 percent rate. Naturally, he got the miners' business.

Unlike his victims, however, Sharon had the financial

wherewithal to explore further and tap into the mines' potential. The Bank of California controlled a dozen Comstock mines and operated several stamp mills as well — which Sharon forced mine operators to use, increasing his profits.

In the words of Dan De Quille, Twain's colleague at the *Enterprise*, Sharon "had the nerve to advance money for the development of mines and the building of mills at a time when no outside banking-house would have ventured a cent. He saw that, though some of the mining companies were in 'borrasca' [unproductive] there was every likelihood of them being in 'bonanza' again soon, provided they were furnished with a sum sufficient to make proper explorations."

One of Sharon's few miscalculations came when the Bank of California sold the Consolidated Virginia mine to Mackay's group. Sharon, who despised "those Irishmen," thought he'd sold them a tapped-out mine, having spent more than $1 million on exploring there without return.

The Irishmen pumped $200,000 more into the project without result, but then hit the mother lode: a 50-foot-wide vein at the heart of the Comstock. It was the "Big Bonanza" that transformed them into the Silver Kings.

That misstep aside, Sharon could seemingly do no wrong. His climb to the top of the financial heap was complete when his boss, Ralston, was ruined in 1875 by a stock crash just weeks after he'd spent $5 million to build the Palace Hotel in San Francisco. Ralston died that same year, and Sharon took his place as bank president.

He also became the principal owner of the Palace Hotel.

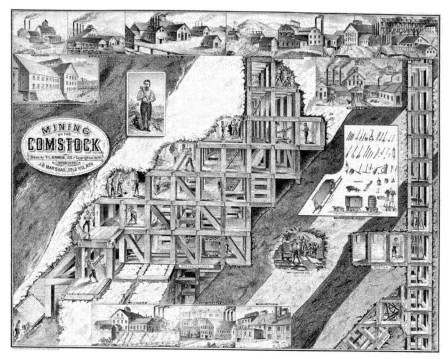

This 1876 illustration titled "Mining the Comstock" shows drawings of several mining operations, including the Ophir and Consolidated Virginia. *Library of Congress*

Much of this occurred after Twain left Virginia City, but his colleague De Quille, who continued working for the *Enterprise*, pointed out in his book *The Big Bonanza* that Sharon tightened his grip on the Comstock by financing construction of the Virginia & Truckee Railroad, using $500,000 in public funds to start construction, then mortgaging it to complete the project.

"In this way," De Quille wrote, "he built the road without putting his hand into his own pocket for a cent, and he still owns half the road — worth $2,500,000 and bringing in, as Mr. Adolph Sutro says, $12,000 per day."

Sharon tightened his grip on Virginia City further when he bought the *Enterprise* (which had opposed his 1872 candidacy for

U.S. Senate) and won election in his second try.

Sutro, architect of the tunnel that bears his name and later mayor of San Francisco, was one of the few men to stand up to Sharon. Another was Conrad Wiegand, whose crusade against corruption in the area was inspired in part by Sutro — even if he was tilting at windmills.

William Sharon owned the V&T Railroad. Seen here: the railroad depot in Gold Hill. *Author photo*

An assayer who arrived at the end of 1863, Wiegand worked briefly for Gould & Curry before opening the Gold Hill Assay Office two years later.

Wiegand had come from San Francisco, where he'd formed a friendship with Ralston. He was thus able to secure a $19,000 loan from the Bank of California to open the office. But in the Comstock, he was no longer dealing with Ralston, but the bank's local agent, Sharon, who waltzed into Wiegand's office one day with the county sheriff and demanded immediate repayment of the loan.

Unable to satisfy the debt on such short notice, Wiegand

watched helplessly as the sheriff seized his assay equipment as payment, forcing the office to close. Wiegand would find new financing and reopen, but his business was damaged and he never forgot the harm Sharon had caused.

In 1870, he started a newspaper called the *People's Tribune*, with the goal of promoting the "betterment of all things, to the defense of right and the people" and becoming "a conscience to Washoe."

Within two weeks of publishing its first issue, Wiegand found himself accused of libel by the superintendent of the Yellow Jacket Mine, John B. Winters (the same John Winters who had run a stamp mill in Como some years previously). Wiegand had, indeed, made some strong accusations:

"That Wm. Sharon, the Board of Trustees, or John B. Winters are indictable before the Grand Jury for offenses of omission and commission of which, if convicted, that fact would go far to purify the atmosphere of the state."

When he didn't get a retraction, Winters demanded a meeting, and Wiegand consented to one at 4 p.m. in his office. When Winters didn't show up, Wiegand was about ready to leave when *Gold Hill News* editor Phillip Lynch arrived and said Winters wanted to meet at the *News* office instead. Winters wasn't there, either, but he was waiting in the basement when Lynch led Wiegand down there.

It was, Wiegand later said in a letter to the *Enterprise*, "admirably adapted in the proper hands to the purposes of murder."

Winters demanded a written retraction, and Wiegand refused, whereupon Winters lost it, hitting the other man repeatedly with a cowhide and knocking him senseless.

It was the second attack on Wiegand in just a few days.

In the earlier assault, Wiegand had been waylaid on the street in Gold Hill by a man named Griff Williams, who'd knocked him down and left him with a black eye in retaliation for Wiegand allegedly "talking about him" — which Wiegand denied. Williams pleaded guilty, was fined $7.50, and released.

But suspicion for the attacks fell on Sharon, who'd been criticized along with Winters in the *People's Tribune*. The banker, perhaps seeking to deflect blame for the attacks on Wiegand, may have used his clout as a board member of the Yellow Jacket Mine Co. to have Winters terminated from his position.

Wiegand's crusading brand of journalism brought a mixed response. The *Reno Crescent* suggested that he might inaugurate a movement that would "sweep the state," while the *White Pine News* condemned him, saying he wanted to be "independent of all kinds of responsibility for his words and acts, and has for a long time acted independently of all the rules of common sense."

Lynch of the *Gold Hill News* condemned Winters' attack, but at the same time defended him: "Winters is very mad just now," he told Wiegand, "but when he is himself, he is one of the finest men I ever met. In fact, he told me the reason he did not meet you upstairs was to spare you the humiliation of a beating in the sight of others."

Yet perhaps the most interesting response came from Mark Twain.

He hadn't been in Nevada for a couple of years, and hadn't been at the *Enterprise* for six, but his old boss, editor Joe Goodman, had waded into the fray by defending Wiegand, stating that he simply wasn't capable of violence or rancor: "Mr. Wiegand is a weak man, and notoriously non-combative," he wrote.

Twain, in the process of writing *Roughing It*, used that venue to second the motion, calling Wiegand a "harmless man" and a "gentle spirit" — even if he was a trifle full of himself. ("If ever there was an oyster that fancied itself a whale... or a zephyr that deemed itself a hurricane, it is Conrad Wiegand.")

"When I met Conrad, he was Superintendent of the Gold Hill Assay Office — and he was not only its Superintendent, but its entire force. And he was a street preacher, too, with a mongrel religion of his own invention, whereby he expected to regenerate the universe. This was years ago.

"Here latterly he has entered journalism; and his journalism is what it might be expected to be: colossal to the ear, but pigmy to the eye. It is extravagant grandiloquence confined to a newspaper about the size of a double letter sheet. He doubtless edits, sets the type, and prints his paper, all alone; but he delights to speak of the concern as if it occupies a block and employs a thousand men."

The *People's Tribune* lasted just six issues.

Piper's Payment Plan

One early Virginia City business was the John Piper Old Corner Bar, which was operating by 1861 at B and Union streets. Those familiar with the city may recognize the Piper name as belonging to the famed opera house that sits on that corner today — and houses the modern Corner Bar.

John Piper came to Virginia City from San Francisco in 1860 purchased the opera house, then located on D Street between Union and Taylor, after original owner Tom Maguire in 1867 was beset with financial problems. Piper, who'd worked at Maguire's Opera House in San Francisco, already owned the property where the opera house was located. He completed the purchase with financial backing from Comstock tycoon John Mackay and promptly renamed the building Piper's Opera House.

It was in this building that Twain presented a lecture on Halloween night of 1866 (when it was still Maguire's), returning two years later for a two-night engagement in April. But you can no longer visit the place where Twain appeared, with its four private boxes, parquet and orchestra apartments: It burned in the Great Fire of 1875, after which Piper rebuilt in its present location on B Street.

C Street before the Great Fire of 1875 shows Maguire's Opera House as the tall building, second from foreground on the right. *Joe Curtis collection*

That structure would burn in another fire eight years later, and the current opera house opened there in 1875.

Although Twain appeared three times at the opera house, he was a far more frequent visitor to the Piper's Corner Bar. As a man who enjoyed his alcohol, he doubtless frequented other establishments, too, perhaps including the Union Brewery on C Street, which was established in 1863. With more than four dozen drinking establishments in the city, there were plenty from which to choose.

CHAS. BAKER,
UNION BREWERY
40 North C Street,
VIRGINIA.

Today's iteration of the Union Brewery on C Street, which was founded in 1863 and rebuilt twice, after fires in 1865 and 1875.
Author photo

But Piper's appears to have been his favorite watering hole, and may well have been the place where he acquired his famous *nom de plume.* Indeed, an 1877 story from the *Eureka (Nevada) Sentinel* suggests that the way John Piper ran a tab at his bar provided Sam Clemens with the inspiration for his pen name.

"We knew Clemens in the early days and know exactly how he came to be dubbed 'Mark Twain,'" the story states. "John Piper's saloon on B street used to be the grand rendezvous for all the Virginia City Bohemians. Piper conducted a cash business and refused to keep any books. As a special favor, however, he would occasionally chalk down drinks to the boys, on the wall back of the bar.

"Sam Clemens, when localizing for the *Enterprise*, always had an account, with the balance against him, on Piper's wall. ... Most of his drinking was conducted in singlehanded contests, but occasionally he would invite Dan De Quille, Charley Parker, Bob Lowery, or Al Doten, never more than one of them, however, at a time, and whenever he did, his invariable parting injunction to Piper was to 'Mark Twain,' meaning two chalkmarks, of course."

Twain himself denied this, maintaining New Orleans Picayune writer Isaiah Sellers had originally used the name.

"He died in 1869," Twain declared, "and as he could no longer need that signature, I laid violent hands upon it without asking permission of the proprietor's remains. That is the history of the nom de plume I bear."

It's a colorful story, as Twain's typically are. But there's a big problem with his explanation: He began using the name in 1863, while working for the Enterprise, six years *before* the date of Sellers' death. Besides, there's no record of Sellers ever using it in the first place.

The Fireman

Twain embarked on a trip to San Francisco in May of 1863 with his friend and rival Clement T. Rice (whom he had nicknamed "The Unreliable," his counterpart at the *Virginia Union*). Both covered the Territorial Legislature.

A May 3 column in the *Territorial Enterprise* said Twain "had gone to display his ugly person and disgusting manners and wildcat on Montgomery Street. In all of which he will be assisted by his protégée, the Unreliable."

While in San Francisco, Twain stayed at the Occidental Hotel, and during his time there, he became acquainted with a firefighter he met at the Blue Wing Saloon on Montgomery Street, where they'd swap stories over drinks.

"Sam was a dandy, he was," the firefighter recalled 35 years later — by which time he was the owner of his own saloon, the Gotham. "He could drink more than any feller I ever seen."

People would keep buying him drinks, and he'd keep talking.

"Once he started, he'd set there till morning telling yarns," provided someone would throw a bowl at him every few minutes. He beat the record for lyin' — nobody was in a race with him there..."

Twain hit it off so well with his new drinking buddy that he invited the firefighter to Virginia City, where they hung out at a popular saloon called the Sazerac at 10 South C Street, which was owned by Tom Peasley. It was a natural choice, since Peasley was a firefighter himself: In fact, he was the fire chief, having organized the Virginia City Volunteer Fire Department.

According to Clemens' visiting friend, it was at the Sazerac, rather than at Piper's, that Clemens acquired his pen name. The story of how it came about was similar to the one told by Doten — except in this case, it was because Clemens was a cheapskate.

He'd been putting off paying Peasley what he owed, which might not have been such a good idea. Peasley, who also managed Maguire's Opera House for a couple of years, had a reputation as a tough guy with a hot temper. But another man, Larry Ryan, was tending bar that day. So Clemens decided he'd use the same tactic to get a couple of free drinks that he'd used on Peasley. After he ordered cocktails for himself and the firefighter, Ryan stood there, expecting payment. But Clemens just held up two fingers and pointed to the slate, indicating he wanted to run a tab. "Larry," he said, "mark twain."

(That can't have been the first time it had happened: Clemens had first used the name "Mark Twain" in a letter published February 3, three months before he left for San Francisco. But early the next year, whether by coincidence or not, Clement T. Rice wrote a column in the *Union* referring to Clemens as "Mark Two.")

The day after their meeting at Peasley's place, the firefighter returned to San Francisco. He said he never saw Clemens again, but that his friend had told him something that stuck with him: "One day, he says to me, 'I am going to put you between the covers of a book some of these days...'"

The firefighter told him to go ahead, "but don't disgrace my name."

He didn't.

Years later, Twain sent the firefighter a copy of a book he had written, and there was his name right on the cover in the title: *The Adventures of Tom Sawyer*.

Artemus Ward

Someone else who used a nom de plume — and who appeared at the Opera House — turned out to be not only an inspiration but a catalyst to Twain's career.

Ward's real name was Charles Farrar Browne, and he is thought to have been the world's first stand-up comedian. Like Twain, he began his career in newspapers, publishing a series of articles in the *Cleveland Plain Dealer*. And like Twain, he regaled his readers with tales that weren't always exactly... true.

In February of 1858, for instance, he wrote that a hyena had escaped from its confinement in a circus cage and was terrorizing the good people of Paulding County. Paulding was sufficiently distant from Cleveland (just short of 180 miles) that it was unlikely that anyone would check on the veracity of the story. So the details, which captivated Ward's readers, were generally assumed to be true. If they seemed farfetched, it just made for a more riveting tale.

According to Ward's account of the Paulding County hyena, a group of men seeking to recapture it finally tracked it to the local cemetery, where they surrounded it. But "the monster" leapt at them, striking one of them with a fatal blow before escaping into the woods, reportedly killing a second man in the process (though this had not been confirmed). Two men and a boy were knocked down, but not seriously injured by the hyena, which was "said to be the largest one of its species in America."

After readers waited for three days with bated breath to find out what happened to the hyena, they were "re-Ward-ed" with a retraction instead. The *Plain Dealer* (which clearly hadn't been so plain in its dealing this time) fessed up to "a few errors" in the story. First off, no one had been killed by the hyena. Second, the hyena had never escaped its cage, for the simple reason that, third, it didn't exist. "He is not there now, never was there, and it is firmly believed, will never be again," the article stated emphatically. It did, however, stand by one unassailable fact: There was, in fact, a place called Paulding County.

Ward, who rose rapidly to become editor of *Vanity Fair* in New York, came to the Comstock in 1863, and Twain announced the comedian's pending visit with a comic November 27 column of the *Enterprise*.

Ward traveled east to Virginia City from San Francisco with

his manager, E.P. Hingston, reaching Sacramento via steamboat, Folsom by rail, and taking a stage over Johnson Pass to Carson City, where he gave a lecture.

When he got to Virginia City, he stayed about a week, and according to Hingston, "formed many new acquaintances, with some of whom acquaintance ripened into warm friendship. Among the later was Mr. Samuel L. Clemens, now well known as 'Mark Twain.'"

ARTEMUS WARD
AT GOLD HILL
—IN—
VESEY'S HALL,
—ON—
THURSDAY EVENING, DEC. 24th,
(Christmas Eve).

Admission - - - One Dollar.

☞ TICKETS—To be had of Mr. Vesey, at the Hotel, and at the doors in the evening.
☞ Doors open at 7; Commence at 8 o'clock.
de24 2t

This ad for Artemus Ward's appearance at Vesey's appeared in the *Gold Hill News*.

Twain took him on an underground tour of the Gould & Curry Mine before he gave a performance called "Babes in the Woods" on December 22 at Maguire's Opera House to an audience made up mostly of miners.

Plans called for Ward to appear at Vesey's in Gold Hill on Christmas Eve, and he was spotted in Virginia City the day before that scheduled show, enjoying a drink with "the most witty writer in this territory." That was according to the *Gold Hill Daily News*... which was referring not to Twain, but to Dan De Quille. "Dan De Quille and Artemus Ward!" the *News* crowed. To see the two tipping glasses together! 'Tis worth five dollars to see it."

No mention of Twain at all.

But Twain was in the thick of the holiday shenanigans involving Ward, De Quille, and *Enterprise* editor Joe Goodman. After an appearance by Ward in Silver City, the three convened

Artemus Ward and Mark Twain both appeared at the first Piper's (Maguire's) Opera House on C Street. After two fires, it was rebuilt on B Street. That building is seen here in the 19th century, top, and 2022. *Joe Curtis Collection; author photo*

after midnight for an oyster supper along with Hingston and *Enterprise* co-owner Denis McCarthy (later Twain's road manager).

By Goodman's account, they ate and drank, with one glass of wine following on the heels of another, until dawn was breaking. Then Ward declared, "I can't walk the earth. I feel like walking on the skies, but as I can't, I'll walk on the roofs."

So they did just that, climbing up a shed and cavorting along the tops of one-story houses, leaping from roof to roof.

At the end of it all, Ward was seen feeding Twain mustard from a spoon, astride a barrel on the porch of Fred Getzler's saloon. Somehow, Ward managed to give a lecture, as scheduled, that evening.

In fact, however, newspapers in the Comstock seemed in competition to get in Ward's good graces. If those were its intentions, however, the *Virginia Union* failed miserably. The newspaper sent an editor by the name of Pepper to the International Hotel, where Ward was staying in the loft. The man, however, was intoxicated, and Ward was doubtful as to his true identity.

"What name?" he asked.

But Pepper (at least according to Ward) was so inebriated he'd forgotten.

He left, and Ward reported hearing him spend the next 10 minutes pacing up and down in the hallway outside before finally returning with the answer: "Pepper!"

There was indeed a Pepper employed as editor in Virginia City at the time, according to the 1864 mercantile guide, so at least that portion of the story rings true. Upon recalling his name, Pepper became so satisfied with himself that he repeated it several times, laughed at himself, then promptly departed. He didn't return.

"I had often heard of a man being 'so drunk that he didn't know what town he lived in,' but here was a man so hideously intoxicated that he didn't know what his name was. I saw him no more, but I heard from him, for he published a notice of my lecture in which he said I had 'a dissipated air.'"

Adding insult to insult, it further referred to him as "a mercenary clown."

With the *Enterprise* staff, on the other hand, he was fast friends. Writing to Twain ("My Dearest Love") from Austin on New Year's Day, Ward asked him to pass along his "love to Jo Goodman and Dan" De Quille, thanking the newspaper for its favorable review.

"Your notice, by the way, did much good here, as it doubtless will elsewhere. The miscreants of the *Union* will be batted on the snout if they ever dare pollute this rapidly rising city [Austin] with their loathsome presence."

Ward went on from there to Salt Lake City on the Pioneer Company stage. He saw talent in Twain and promised to put in a good word for him with his friends at the *New York Sunday Mercury*. Twain sent along several articles, which were in fact published, but his big break came when Ward asked him for a contribution to Ward's planned book called *Travels*.

That volume was in fact published, in 1865, but you won't find anything from Twain in it. His proposed contribution, based on a tale he'd heard from a bartender in the California gold country town of Angels Camp, was titled "Jim Smiley and His Jumping Frog." Unfortunately, Twain dickered around with the story too long, and Ward's book had already gone to press by the time he sent it, so Ward forwarded it instead to the *New York Sunday Press*, which published it.

The story proved so popular it was reprinted a number of times, and Bret Harte published a revised version called "The

Celebrated Jumping Frog of Calaveras County" in *The Californian* later that year. Twain used it as the linchpin of his first book, a collection of 27 previously published stories that appeared in 1867 under the title *The Celebrated Jumping Frog of Calaveras County, and Other Sketches.*

Sadly, Ward died of tuberculosis on a lecture tour in London some four years after that, at just 34 years of age. Recalling his old friend years later, Twain called him "one of the kindest and gentlest men in the world," adding that, "the hold which he took on the Londoners surpasses imagination."

"To this day one of the first questions which a Londoner asks me is if I knew Artemus Ward. The answer, 'yes,' makes that man my friend on the spot. Artemus seems to have been on the warmest terms with thousands of those people. Well, he seems never to have written a harsh thing against anybody — neither have I, for that matter — at least nothing harsh enough for a body to fret about — and I think he never felt bitter toward people.

"There may have been three or four other people like that in the world at one time or another, but they probably died a good while ago. I think his lecture on the 'Babes in the Wood' was the funniest thing I ever listened to."

Standing at the Gallows

Twain's return to Virginia City in 1866 was triumphant.

Alf Doten, editor of the *Virginia Daily Union**, noted that his 90-minute-plus lecture on the Sandwich Islands at Maguire's Opera House drew a "crammed house" and was "mighty good," labeling it an "immense success."

He returned again in 1868.

But a week before he took the stage on that second visit, he had occasion to witness justice executed in one of its most brutal forms: the hanging of convicted murderer John Millian.

"I never had witnessed an execution before, and did not believe I could be present at this one without turning away my head at the last moment," he wrote. "But I did not know what fascination there was about the thing, then. I only went because I thought I ought to have a lesson, and because I believed that if ever it would be possible to see a man hanged, and derive satisfaction from the spectacle, this was the time."

Millian's victim hadn't been just anyone. He'd killed the famous prostitute Julia Bulette, who had earned a reputation as the proverbial "hooker with a heart of gold." Indeed, the *Territorial Enterprise* once described her as having a "kind-hearted, liberal, benevolent and charitable disposition."

She'd come to town in the early 1860s, drifting east after working as a prostitute in various California mining camps, and lived in a small dwelling she rented at D and Union streets in the city's red-light district.

Bulette earned her way into the good graces of Virginia City residents by helping out the fire department — an essential institution then, as now, and even more so in a time and place that fires were commonplace (the Great Fire of 1875 being only the most prominent example). She actively fought fires herself, even working the brakes on hand pumpers, and was also said to have served on soup lines during flu outbreaks.

Twain's friend Alf Doten wrote about being caught up in the holiday spirit in 1865, when he partied at Bulette's whorehouse and went to bed drunk at 2 or 3 in the morning. The following June, she threw a ball, and he was in attendance, and he reported on Millian's trial for her murder.

Her popularity was attested by the response to the guilty

verdict. "This is the first instance I ever knew, of public rejoicing over such a verdict, where a man's life was at stake," Doten wrote.

The evidence was "purely circumstantial, but overwhelming," he said, noting that the jury took just 90 minutes before returning with their answer. (Millian had been found possessing some of her belongings, including a dress pattern she'd ordered, and, according to Twain, had been discovered by another woman under that woman's house, waiting with a knife to ambush her.)

"When the verdict was announced, the bell of No 1 pealed out in notes of joy — No 2 responded, and then some of the steam whistles sounded, thinking it was alarm of fire... Jule Bulette was an honorary member of Va Engine Co No 1 at the time of her death, hence the bell ringing."

Millian appealed to the Nevada Supreme Court, but the justices left the verdict intact, clearing the way for his execution.

Twain, no longer working for the *Enterprise*, filed a report on the hanging for the *Chicago Republican*. He didn't mention Bulette by name, but it's likely he would have known her. She was the favorite of Tom Peasley, the fire chief and owner of the saloon where Twain and Tom Sawyer once swapped stories and drinks.

Regardless of any possible personal connection, Twain was clearly in favor of the execution. Millian, he wrote, was "no common murderer — else he would have gone free. He was a heartless assassin" who had lain in wait under the victim's home "knocked her senseless with a billet of wood as she slept and then strangled her with his fingers."

"He carried off all her money, her watches, and every article of her wearing apparel, and the next day, with quiet effrontery, put some crepe on his arm and walked in her funeral procession."

According to one count, as many as 4,000 people attended the hanging. Twain was one of them.

"I saw it all," he reported. "I took exact note of every detail, even to [Millian's] considerately helping to fix the leather strap that bound his legs together and his quiet removal of his slippers — and I never wish to see it again. I can see that stiff, straight corpse hanging there yet, with its black pillow-cased head turned rigidly to one side, and the purple streaks creeping through the hands and driving the fleshy hue of life before them. Ugh!"

*Note: The *Virginia Daily Union* ceased publication in 1867, when it was purchased by the editor of the *Humboldt Register* and rechristened the *Trespass*. It was shortly thereafter purchased again and moved to Hamilton in White Pine County (the new Nevada boomtown), where it stayed in business until 1870.

Getting to Virginia City

U.S. 50 — Turn north from Highway 50 onto Nevada Route 341, then continue north past Silver City on NR 342 past Gold Hill. It's a total of about 5 miles uphill on a well-paved asphalt road.

Key Sites in Virginia City

Bank of California *(Ponderosa Saloon)* — 106 South C St.
Douglas Building *(Washoe Club)* — 112 South C St.
Gould & Curry offices *(Mackay Mansion)* — 291 South D St.
International Hotel site *(mural)* — Union and C streets
Old Corner Bar — 12 North B St.
Tahoe House Hotel — 164 South C St.
Territorial Enterprise — 2-98 South C St.
Union Brewery — 63 C St.

Washoe City.

Reno is the county seat of Washoe County today, but that wasn't the case in Twain's day.

Washoe City, founded in 1860, held that honor. It was a thriving frontier town, built as a foothill camp to provide needed lumber for the Comstock. In fact, it boomed so big that the town had 6,000 residents by the middle of the decade, around the time Twain moved on to California.

Founded: **1860**
Location: **Washoe County**
Population (1865): **6,000**
Elevation: **5,062**
Status: **Semi-ghost town***

* Washoe Valley had a 2020 population of 3,086

Sam Clemens took a stage out to Washoe City three days before Christmas in 1862 for something called the Grand Bull Drivers' Convention.

His account for the *Territorial Enterprise* provided a glimpse at the severity of the winter weather in the region. "The weather was delightful," he wrote sarcastically. "It snowed the entire day. The wind blew such a hurricane that the coach drifted sideways from one toll road to another, and sometimes utterly refused to mind her helm. It is a fearful thing to be at sea in a stagecoach."

The party had hoped to arrive by 4 in the afternoon, but the roads were in such poor condition that the stage broke a spring and was delayed a couple of hours for repairs.

The old Washoe City Jail, now a Garden Center, is the only building to survive from Twain's era in the former Washoe County seat. *Author photo*

One of the speakers, a judge named John Lovejoy, argued for more toll roads, claiming that the competition would keep prices affordable, and several other speakers also addressed the session. After that, the partying began in earnest, with everyone in attendance kicking up their heels in a dance called the quadrille (performed by four couples in a rectangle and similar to a square dance).

"I did not observe any wallflowers," Twain wrote. "The climate of Washoe appears to be unsuited to that kind of vegetation."

The champagne flowed freely, as well, and Lovejoy — who was president of the Paiute Association — could be seen dancing a war dance around a spittoon by evening's end. Twain blamed a friend of his whom he referred to as "The Unreliable" for his own intoxicated state, "for he drank until he lost all sense of etiquette. I actually found myself in bed with him with my boots on."

He was not too badly hung over, however, to file a report of the evening's events with *The Enterprise* the following day.

Sportswriter

Twain's assignments ran the gamut, including athletics. In the fall of 1863, he covered a horserace in Carson City as part of the first Washoe Agricultural, Mining, and Mechanical Society Fair. And on September 23, he went out to cover a prizefight in Washoe Valley at the racetrack there.

These were the days of bareknuckle fights, when rounds didn't end until one fighter put the other on the mat, and the bout in question matched a certain Tom Daly against an opponent named Billy McGrath.

The fight was illegal — Nevada wouldn't legalize prizefighting until 1897, when Carson City hosted the heavyweight title fight between Jim Corbett and Bob Fitzsimmons — but it was still news. So Twain was there to cover it, and he did so in very much the same way online sources do today, with a round-by-round description (but, of course, not in real time).

McGrath scored a knockdown in the first round with "a slinger" to his "jowl." Apparently, however, these contests were as much wrestling as boxing: McGrath ended the seventh round by "falling on" Daly, and most rounds were decided when one man threw the other, rather than knocking him down.

Daly won the fight in the 14th round when McGrath sent Daly toward the mat, then unleashed a glancing uppercut as he was falling. Daly immediately cried foul, and the referee concurred, stopping the bout then and there to declare Daly the victor. Twain clearly did not agree:

"The fact is," he wrote, "Daly was standing square before McGrath when the last blow was struck, and the blow which was ruled a 'foul' never reached its mark, but just grazed Daly's face."

McGrath wasn't happy, but those who'd bet on him were even more outraged. One of them by the name of Harry Lazarus began cursing the referee's decision, and a Daly backer named Maldonado responded by insisting that the blow had been a foul. "Lazarus called him a liar," Twain reported, "and pistols were immediately drawn."

And fired.

Other shots quickly rang out, and the crowd began to panic. Horses were spooked, and two of them were shot in the melee. With a thousand or more fans in attendance, a confused scene ensued that, according to Twain, beggared all description. When the dust cleared, both Lazarus and Maldonado were lying on tables at an adjacent saloon. Lazarus wasn't seriously hurt, but Maldonado had been hit multiple times. Two of his fingers had been shattered and would need to be amputated, and, while he was still alive when Twain departed at 4 in the afternoon, Maldonado "was not expected to survive long."

No wonder boxing was illegal.

Twain's colleague Dan De Quille reported on another prizefight October 11 in *The Golden Era*, a San Francisco literary journal to which Twain also contributed. This one took place below the Gould & Curry Mill, matching two unrelated men named Bradley — Pat and Jack — in a grudge match to settle an old quarrel.

"They stripped to the waist and went at it in grim earnest," De Quille wrote, "no throwing off or fooling around."

After several rounds spanning 36 minutes, Pat declined to continue. Though he was the larger and heavier of the two combatants, he had taken a severe beating, and one of his eyes was swollen shut. Both Bradleys were covered with blood, and one observer remarked that the fight made the Daly-McGrath scrap seem like "child's play" in comparison.

Twain reportedly called it the "severest fight that has ever taken place in the Territory."

Despite the brutality of it all, Twain seemed quite comfortable with "the manly art." So much so that he even used it as material for a satire on the political gamesmanship between California Governor Leland Stanford and the governor-elect, F.F. Low, which he portrayed in the form of an imaginary prize fight with a $100,000 purse.

His round-by-round account of the made-up match included a vivid description of Low as having "grabbed Stanford by the hair of the head, swung him thrice round and round in the air like a lasso, and then slammed him on the ground with such mighty force that he quivered all over, and squirmed painfully, like a worm."

In the end, both men threw in the towel — or in this case, the sponge — simultaneously, and neither got the better of the other.

Twain concluded by apologizing "in the most abject manner" to the governor and governor-elect. "It is not possible for me to say how I ever managed to believe that refined and educated gentlemen like these could stoop to engage in the loathsome and degrading pastime of prize-fighting."

But somehow, he did. And, apparently, he had a grand time doing it.

Getting to Washoe City

U.S. 395 Alternate — Turn off Interstate 580 onto U.S. 395 Alternate, which parallels the interstate. Washoe City is on U.S. 395 Alternate south of Eastlake Boulevard.

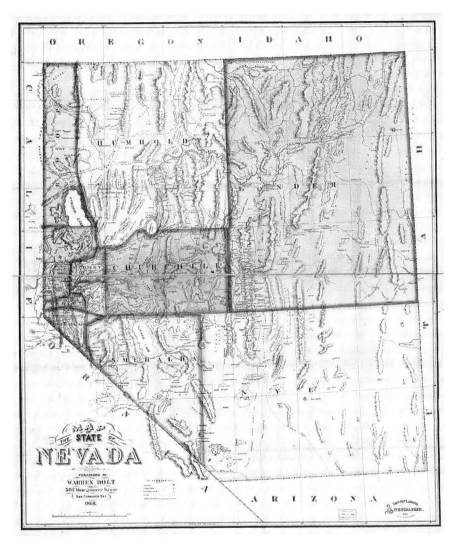

This map shows Nevada as it looked upon gaining statehood. Note that some counties that exist today, such as Pershing, White Pine, Lincoln, Eureka, Mineral, and Elko, do not exist, having not yet been carved out of the original counties. Also note that the bottom section of the state is still a part of Arizona.

Contemporaries.

Some of the people in Mark Twain's Nevada whom he interacted, wrote about, or who helped shape his world.

Ambrose, Nicholas.

"Dutch Nick," as he was known, founded the first hotel-saloon in Empire, on the Carson River, just east of Carson City, where he dispensed his own brew called tarantula whiskey. The riverside location made the place prone to flooding, and the river damaged Dutch Nick's in 1862 and again in 1868. A Prussian immigrant born in 1824, he filed a land claim in 1855 and, by the following year, owned 373 acres of land in Eagle Valley. He also opened a saloon in Gold Hill, the first frame structure built there. While the town of Empire is gone, Ambrose's red brick house still stands near the golf course, and he's buried at the cemetery there. Ambrose died in 1880 of tuberculosis. His establishment is mentioned in Twain's fictional account of "A Bloody Massacre in Carson Canyon."

Bulette, Julia (Jule).

Prostitute and volunteer firefighter in Virginia City who arrived in the early 1860s and was murdered in 1867. John Millian was convicted of killing her and sentenced to be hanged. Twain witnessed his execution while in Virginia City on a speaking tour in 1868.

Burch, John C.

Member of the "Irish Brigade" and an assistant Indian agent to Governor James Nye. He named a stream in the Tahoe area for himself, which today is instead called Marlette Creek.

Clagett, William H.

Lawyer from New York who moved to Carson City in 1861, the same year Samuel Clemens arrived. To Clemens, he was "Billy." Clemens once sold him a black horse with a white face for $45.

Clagett joined Clemens and two others on their fortune-hunting trip to Unionville. Although they failed to find gold or silver there, Clagett stayed for a while and set up a law practice there. He later moved back to Virginia City, where he also practiced law. Clagett served as a member of the Territorial House of Representatives in 1862 and 1863 before moving to the Nevada Assembly in 1864 and '65, where he introduced a bill to make American City the state capital. He later moved to Montana, and served in the U.S. House of Representatives for one term. During that time he introduced legislation that paved the way for the creation of Yellowstone National Park. He went back to practicing law after that, and died in 1901.

Clemens, Jennie.

Daughter and only child of Orion and Mollie Clemens, Jennie was born in 1855 and attended Sierra Seminary in Carson City. She contracted spotted fever in 1864 and died of meningitis a few days later. At the time of her death, she had been saving money to buy a pulpit Bible for the Presbyterian Church. She is buried in Carson City at Lone Mountain Cemetery.

Clemens, Orion.

Elder brother of Samuel Clemens, he was born in Tennessee and moved with his family to Hannibal, Missouri, as a teenager. In 1847, bought the *Hannibal Journal* newspaper, which employed his younger brother. In 1853, he moved to Iowa, where he ran the *Muscatine Journal* for a year, and was appointed secretary of the Nevada Territory by President Lincoln in 1861. After leaving office, he served briefly in the state Assembly, but struggled financially and was forced to leave Nevada in 1866. His home in Carson City still stands. Orion Clemens died in 1897.

Clemens, Mollie.

Wife of Orion Clemens and Mark Twain's sister-in-law, Mary "Mollie" Clemens was born Mary Eleanor Stotts 1834 in Illinois. She married Orion Clemens 20 years later. After her husband died in 1897, Twain supported her until her death in 1904.

Coulter, J.E.

Member of the "Irish Brigade," he later served as a member of the Nevada Assembly in 1877.

Curry, Abraham.

Carson City pioneer who opened a pair of hotels there (the Great Basin and Warm Springs) and was perhaps the city's most prominent citizen during the 1860s and early '70s. He also founded the Gould & Curry Mine with Alva Gould in 1859. The Nevada Legislature held meetings at both of his hotels, and he became both the first warden of Nevada State Prison, on land he sold to the state, and superintendent of the Carson City Mint, which was built from stones quarried at the prison. His last major project was to build the engine shop and machine shop in Carson City for the Virginia & Truckee Railroad. He died of a stroke in 1873.

De Quille, Dan.

Pen name for William Wright, an Ohio native who came to Virginia City in 1859 and was a colleague of Mark Twain's at the *Territorial Enterprise*. The two stayed in touch after Twain left Nevada, and Twain provided him with advice on publishing his book,

History of Big Bonanza, in 1876. Twain wrote an introduction to the book and got De Quille a contract with his own publisher to produce it. De Quille stayed with the *Enterprise* until it closed in 1893 and died in 1898.

Doten, Alfred.

A carpenter, miner, musician, and newspaperman, Doten was born in Massachusetts and spent 13 years looking for gold in California before moving to Nevada. He was a contributor for the *Como Sentinel* and *Virginia Daily Union*, becoming its editor in 1864. He later worked as an editorial writer for the *Territorial Enterprise* and as editor of the *Gold Hill News* until 1881, when he left to edit the *Reese River Reveille* in Austin, Nevada. He was married in an open boat on Lake Tahoe in 1874 and died in Carson City in 1903 at the age of 74. His extensive journals touch on some of Mark Twain's activities.

Fair, James G.

One of the four "Silver Kings" of the Comstock, "Slippery Jim" Fair was an Irish immigrant born in 1831 who traveled to the United States as a boy in 1843 and was raised on an Illinois farm. He built a stamp mill on the Carson River and served as mine superintendent in the Comstock before forming a

partnership with John Mackay, James C. Flood, and William S. O'Brien, striking it rich with the Consolidated Mine. Fair built a $50 million fortune and, with Mackay, owned the Nevada Bank of San Francisco, which became the largest bank in America at one time. Their chief rival was the Bank of California, controlled by William Ralston and, later William Sharon. Ironically, Fair succeeded Sharon in the U.S. Senate, where he served from 1881 to 1887. He died at the age of 63 in 1894.

Fitch, Thomas.

Editor of the *Virginia Union*, he challenged *Enterprise* editor Joe Goodman to a duel in August of 1863. The following year, he started a weekly literary journal called the *Occidental*, inviting Twain to contribute a chapter in a planned serialized novel, but the *Occidental* folded before he got the chance. In 1864, Fitch became a lawyer and ran for Congress unsuccessfully. In 1865, he was appointed district attorney of Washoe County, and ran for Congress again four years later, this time winning a seat he held for two years. As an attorney, he defended Brigham Young against polygamy charges and the Earp brothers after the Gunfight at OK Corral.

Gasherie, D.J.

The first elected sheriff of Ormsby County, Gasherie took office by upsetting incumbent William J. Marley in 1862. He remained in office until Timothy G. Smith was elected in 1864 and was in office for most of the time Twain was in the area.

Goodman, Joseph.

Owner and editor of the *Territorial Enterprise*, Goodman hired Sam Clemens as a reporter in 1862. He'd become co-owner of the newspaper a year earlier and soon owned it outright. A native of New York, he traveled to California to work as a typesetter and found himself as owner of the *Enterprise* when he was no more than 23 years of age (so he was younger than Twain when he hired him). Later, in 1872, Goodman took an editorial stand against ruthless banker William Sharon, who was running for U.S. Senate. His opposition bore dividends when Sharon lost, but the banker just bought the newspaper from Goodman, ran again two years later, and won. Goodman later moved to Fresno and Mariposa, where he pursued archaeological research, and died in 1917 at the age of 80.

Gould, Alva.

Born in 1815, he located the Gould & Curry Mine in January of 1859. He partnered with Abraham Curry but sold his stake to George Hearst for a paltry $450. He thought he'd gotten the better end of the deal, and reportedly ran down the street yelling, "I tricked a Californian." But Hearst and his partners made a profit of more than $90,000 in just two months by mining 38 tons of high-grade ore, which they took to California. Hearst sold his share of the mine at a massive profit less than a year after he bought it, while Gould wound up running a peanut stand in Reno two decades later.

Greeley, Horace.

Founder (in 1841) and editor of the *New York Tribune*, Greeley helped start the Republican Party and later waged an unsuccessful campaign for president. Hank Monk drove him on a memorable stage ride to Placerville in 1859. Or did he? Twain, who had heard the story so often he became sick of it, wrote to Greeley in 1871, in an attempt to determine whether the story was actually true. When Greeley failed to respond, he concluded that the story was a fiction and stated as much in *Roughing It*. Whether for this cause or some other reason, Twain doesn't seem to have been particularly fond of Greeley. Later in *Roughing It*, he mocks his poor penmanship, reproducing a letter he wrote (left) concerning turnips, with several absurd translations of his nearly illegible handwriting: He'd meant to say, "Potatoes do sometimes make vines; turnips remain passive: cause unnecessary to state." But it came across as, "Poultices do sometimes choke swine; tulips reduce posterity; causes leather to resist." Or, "Polygamy dissembles majesty; extracts redeem polarity; causes hitherto exist." Greeley died in 1872 at the age of 61, a month after losing the presidential election.

Gridley, Reuel Colt.

Gridley attended school with Mark Twain in Hannibal, Missouri, and later encountered him again in Nevada. In his autobiography, Twain relates that he recognized Gridley's voice when he heard it

in Carson City, even though he hadn't seen him in nearly two decades. Like Twain, he spent some time as a journalist, running a newspaper in Oroville, California, in 1852 before moving to Austin, Nevada, at the time of the silver boom there to start a mercantile on the east end of town. Gridley toured the

country and repeatedly auctioned off a sack of flour to raise money for the Sanitary Commission, which provided aid to injured Union soldiers, but in doing so, he neglected his store in Austin and went broke. The store closed, but the stone building remains. Gridley moved to Stockton, California, after that, but Austin honored him by incorporating his flour sack into its town seal. Gridley died in 1870.

Hearst, George.

Born in 1820 in Missouri, Hearst used his business savvy and good fortune to parlay a pair of mining investments into an actual fortune. First, he bought half of the Gould & Curry Mine, the one

that started Virginia City boom, for a paltry $450. He spent a few hundred dollars more on a stake in the Ophir Mine, which made him even richer. (The Ophir mining camp grew into Silver City.) He built a superintendent's office for Gould & Curry, later known as the Mackay Mansion, but he didn't stay in Virginia City for long. He sold his stake, took nearly $100 million in earnings, and returned to California. His son, William Randolph Hearst became even richer and more famous after taking over the *San Francisco Examiner*, a newspaper George Hearst acquired to settle a gambling debt in 1880. George Hearst served in the California Assembly from 1865 to 1867, and in the U.S. Senate in 1886 and again from 1887 until his death in 1901.

Higbie, Calvin.

Twain's cabinmate in Aurora and partner in the ill-fated Johnson mine venture. Twain dedicated *Roughing It*, his recollections of his time in Nevada, to Higbie, describing him as "an honest man, a genial comrade, and a steadfast friend." Higbie, a civil engineer and conservationist, made one of the first surveys of roads from Nevada to Lake Tahoe. He moved to Plumas County in California sometime around 1880 and died in 1914.

Hopkins, Phillip.

Carson City-area resident and bachelor who was falsely depicted in Mark Twain's fictional article, "A Bloody Massacre in Carson Canyon" as a deranged father of nine who killed his wife and seven of his children before dying of a slit throat. In fact, Hopkins was still very much alive at the time the article was printed.

Ives, John.

Carson City resident who'd come from New York, where he'd been the New York Police Department doctor when future Nevada Governor James Nye was commissioner there. A member of "Captain" John Nye's "Irish Brigade," he was about 50 years old at the time of the Lake Tahoe expedition. He later moved to Aurora, where he was elected to the State Senate, representing Esmeralda County, in 1864.

Kincaid, J.H.

Another member of the "Irish Brigade," Kincaid owned a mercantile at Plaza and Carson streets in Carson City, where he sold dry goods, groceries, clothing, and mining tools, among other items. He lived at the northeast corner of Musser and Nevada streets in the capital and was appointed territorial treasurer by Governor James Nye. Later, he was elected as the third governor of Nevada, serving in that capacity from 1879 until 1882.

Kinney, Johnny.

Companion of Mark Twain on his trip to Lake Tahoe shortly after Twain's arrival in Nevada. Kinney, 22, had lived in Cincinnati, where his father, Eli, owned a bank, before he traveled to Nevada. He would return to Ohio in 1862.

Laird, James.

Editor and owner of the *Virginia Daily Union* whom Mark Twain
once challenged to a duel. Laird remained at the Union until 1866,
when he left for Montana. He later served as a U.S. marshal in the
Dakota Territory and sheriff of Cheyenne County. He came to a
bad end however, in 1869, when a man named Chauncy Baily
discovered Laird in bed with Baily's wife — and shot him.

Luther, Ira M.

A member of the "Irish Brigade," he came to California in 1850 and
to the Carson Valley in 1858. He was about 41 years old at the
time of the Tahoe expedition, and Luther Pass between Lake
Tahoe and Woodfords bears his name.

Mackay, John.

A Dublin native, Irish
immigrant John Mackay
worked the California
gold fields for eight years
before coming to
Virginia City in 1859. He
started off working in a
mine for $4 a day and
eventually bought into
the Kentuck mine,
which made him rich.
He ultimately formed a
partnership with James
G. Fair, James C. Flood,
and William S. O'Brien,

who became known as the "Silver Kings" or "Bonanza Kings" when their Consolidated Mining Company hit the "Big Bonanza" in 1873 — the largest discovery of ore ever in the Comstock and, indeed, in all of North America. Mackay made $50 million off it and established the Bank of Nevada with Fair in San Francisco as a competitor to the previously dominant Bank of California. He later formed the Commercial Cable Company as a rival to Western Union, laying a pair of transatlantic cables. He died of heart failure in 1902. Mackay Mansion in Virginia City, originally offices of the Gould & Curry Mining Company, bears his name. He lived there after losing his home in the Great Fire of 1875.

McCarthy, Denis E.

Co-owner of the *Territorial Enterprise* with Joseph Goodman. Goodman eventually became sole owner, and McCarthy moved to San Francisco. Twain found him there and made him his road manager. He was in on the prank Twain's friends pulled on him, robbing him at gunpoint on the way back to Virginia City from Gold Hill following a lecture there. Managing editor of the *San Francisco Chronicle* in the early 1870s, he purchased the 3-year-old *Virginia Evening Chronicle* in 1875 and increased its circulation from 2,800 to 8,000 copies, making it the state's leading Democratic journal. Born in Australia of Irish descent, McCarthy died of edema in 1885.

Monk, Henry James.

Stage driver who embarked on his chosen career at the age of 12 in upstate New York and moved to California in 1852. There, he began driving for the California State Company between Auburn and Sacramento. Five years later, Hank started working for J.B. Crandall, driving between Placerville and Genoa, continuing when the line changed hands, eventually being owned by Wells Fargo. In a career spanning more than two decades, he also drove for Billy Wilson's company between Carson and Virginia, and for "Doc" Benton between Carson and Glenbrook on Lake Tahoe. He died of pneumonia in Carson City in 1883.

Neary, James.

A speculator who came west with James Nye, he was a member of the "Irish Brigade." He was about 44 at the time of the Tahoe expedition.

Nye, James.

Born in 1815, Nye was a New York lawyer appointed by Abraham Lincoln as Nevada's territorial governor in 1861. Prior to that, he'd served as head of the Metropolitan Board of Police in New York City. After Nevada gained statehood, he was elected to the Senate as a Republican in 1864 and re-elected in 1867, serving for eight years before losing in his second bid for re-election. While Nye was in the Senate, Twain served as his personal secretary for a few months. After leaving office, Nye returned to New York, where he died in White Plains in 1876. An obituary in the New Orleans Republican stated that he had "been afflicted for some years with softening of the brain" and had been "recently lodged in an insane asylum."

Nye, "Captain" John.

Brother of Nevada Governor James Nye, "the Captain" served as leader of the "Irish Brigade" that staked a timber claim at Lake Tahoe. Nye, three years older than his brother, arrived in Placer County, California, in 1849 and lived there until 1861, when his brother was named territorial governor and he moved to Carson City. Like his brother, he'd been involved in politics, serving as mayor of Mobile, Alabama. Twain mentions helping to care for him when he became severely ill with spasmodic rheumatism in 1862. It was a good deed that didn't go unpunished, as it was part of the reason Twain forfeited a claim in Aurora that turned out to be profitable. Nye, who was 48 at the time, recovered and lived nine more years, dying on July 7, 1871, in Washington, D.C.

Nye, Thomas.

Son of "Captain" John Nye and a member of the "Irish Brigade." Thomas, who was 18 or 19 years old at the time, accompanied Clemens on a visit to Lake Tahoe in October of 1861.

Ormsby, Major William.

An early mayor of Genoa, Ormsby moved there in 1857 as an agent of the Pioneer Stage Line. He later moved to Carson City, where he opened a hotel called the Ormsby House in 1860 and took in two daughters of Paiute elder Truckee: Sarah and Elma Winnemucca. (The city of Winnemucca is named for Sarah.) But when Paiute warriors killed a group of five white settlers and burned the Williams Station stage stop, near today's Silver Springs, Ormsby was chosen to lead a group of vigilantes against them. The Paiutes had burned the station while on a mission to rescue two girls from their tribe who had been kidnapped and abused by the stage stop's owners. Ormsby was one of 76 vigilantes killed in the first Battle of Pyramid Lake. He was dead by the time Twain arrived in Nevada, but helped shaped the world in which Sam Clemens moved.

Oliver, A.W.

A judge and close friend of Twain's at Virginia City, he was already there when Twain arrived. His obituary in the *Sausalito News* described the two as "warm friends and inseparable companions." Oliver was one of the four companions who journeyed to Unionville, identified as "Oliphant" in *Roughing It*. A native of Maine, he moved on to California, where he became a principal in Gilroy and superintendent of schools in San Jose. He died in 1921 at the age of 86.

Peasley, Tom.

Peasley owned a saloon called the Sazerac, where the real-life Tom Sawyer visited with Twain when the San Francisco firefighter came to town. Peasley, a heavy drinker himself and a gunman of some repute, was well-known in Virginia City, not just as a saloon owner but as fire chief. In fact, he had organized the Virginia Engine Company No. 1 and Nevada Hook and Ladder Company No. 1 in 1861. He bought the Sazerac Saloon with his brother the following year, and was known to keep company with prostitute Julia Bulette (likely by no coincidence, a big supporter of the fire department). Peasley ran twice for sheriff, losing both times, but was nonetheless known to take the law into his own hands. He once confronted known killer Langford Peel outside the International Hotel and sent a message by bashing his head against a wall. In 1863, he shot and killed a man. Peasley eventually came to a bad end at a saloon, but not his own. He'd gotten into a fight with a Carson City firefighter named Martin Barnhart in February of 1865, which had ended with Peasley shooting Barnhart in the leg. Barnhart had tried to provoke him into a shootout at Glenbrook on Lake Tahoe that summer, but Peasley didn't take the bait. Then, on February 2, 1866, Barnhart confronted Peasley in front of the Ormsby House and shot him twice in the chest without warning. Peasley somehow managed to pull his own gun and fired, hitting Barnhart three times. Both men died.

Phillips, Horatio.

First cabinmate of Sam Clemens in Aurora. The two parted ways after a falling out.

Piper, John.

Early Virginia City resident who opened Piper's Corner Bar and later purchased Maguire's Opera House with financial support from John Mackay, one of the four Virginia City "Bonanza Kings."

The third and final Piper's Opera House has been restored since the 1937 photo at top was taken. Above: The stage as it appears today. *Historic American Buildings Survey; author photo*

A German immigrant born in Hamburg in 1830, he arrived in Virginia City in 1860. He purchased Maguire's Opera House in 1867, but had to rebuild after the Great Fire of 1875 and again after another fire, reopening in 1885. Lily Langtree, Maud Adams, and Mark Twain were among those to perform at the opera house in its various incarnations. Piper also operated the Carson Opera House in Carson City and, in the 1888, leased and ran the McKissick Opera House at Plaza and Sierra streets in Reno. He died in 1897 at the age of 63, and the Corner Bar closed at that time (although a business by that name now operates at the Opera House). His son Edward operated the Virginia City opera house until it closed in 1924.

Rice, Clement T.

Nicknamed "The Unreliable" by Twain, Rice was a reporter for the rival *Virginia Daily Union*. Both covered the Territorial Legislature for their respective newspapers. Though Twain often poked fun at Rice, the two were friends. Rice accompanied Twain on a trip to San Francisco in 1863, arriving in May, with the two staying at the Occidental. In addition to his career as a journalist, Rice worked as registrar in the U.S. Land Office in Carson City from 1862 to 1864. He met up with Twain again in New York City in 1867, having gone into business there after having success as a prospector. But he apparently lost his money, because he was seeking help from Twain getting a job in the 1880s.

Sawyer, Tom.

San Francisco firefighter who claimed to be the inspiration for the title character in Twain's most famous book. He later became the proprietor of The Gotham Saloon at 935 Mission Street. His wife, the mother of his either three or seven sons (two stories in the *San Francisco Call* differ on the number) lived with him in the rooms above the saloon. Born on New Year's Day in 1827, he moved to California at the age of 23 and worked as a marine engineer before helping to organize the volunteer fire department. He met Twain on his trip to San Francisco in 1863 and later paid him a visit in Virginia City.

Sharon, William.

Comstock agent and later president of the Bank of California, notorious for his cutthroat business practices, which helped him accumulate a near-monopoly in the Comstock. The Ohio native built and owned the Virginia & Truckee Railroad and served one term in the U.S. Senate, from 1875 to 1881, but was largely absent from the chamber, missing 90 percent of its votes. He was involved in a relationship with Sarah Althea Hill, a socialite whose older brother lent his name to the California town of Morgan Hill. She claimed to be his wife and sued him based on a marriage contract Sharon said was fraudulent. After Sharon died in 1885, Hill sought to claim his estate based on a handwritten will that was later ruled a forgery. (She later married her attorney, David Terry, a former California chief justice.)

Stewart, William.

U.S. senator from Nevada from 1865 to 1875 and again from 1887 to 1905, he also served as California's attorney general in 1854. Twain was known to poke fun at Stewart as a reporter, but later worked briefly for him in his Washington, D.C., office after leaving Nevada. He didn't take well to the new position,

forging Stewart's frank on personal correspondence and offending constituents. When one asked that a post office be established in a mining camp, Twain responded, "What the mischief do... you want with a post office? If any letters came there, you couldn't read them." On one occasion, he rejected a Treasury Department report on the grounds that it lacked descriptive passages and contained "no heroes, no plot, no pictures — not even wood-cuts." After a short period, Stewart fired him.

Stowe, Amos.

Proprietor of Steamboat Springs Hotel in 1863, when Mark Twain stayed there.

Sutro, Adolph.

Prussian immigrant who served as mayor of San Francisco from 1895 to 1897. But he was perhaps more famous for building the Sutro Tunnel east of Dayton three decades earlier. He shared a stage with Twain on a ride to Dayton, during which he failed to

comprehend Twain's attempt at humor (much to the latter's chagrin). A tobacco salesman in San Francisco before arriving in Virginia City in 1860, he devised a scheme to construct a tunnel that would reduce the threat of flooding by draining water out of the mine shafts. He wasn't able to come up with the money needed to build it, though, until 1869, after a fire erupted in the Yellow Jacket Mine at nearby Gold Hill: At least 35 workers died in Nevada's worst-ever mining disaster. Miners, worried about the prospects of another tragic accident, decided to support Sutro's project . In the end, it cost him $3.5 million and stretched nearly four miles upon completion in 1878. A small town

grew up around the mouth of the tunnel, but Sutro himself returned to San Francisco, where he built a new Victorian-style version of the Cliff House (previous page) in 1896, replacing the first structure, which dated back to 1863. It burned in 1907. Sutro died in 1898.

Tillou, Cornbury S.

Known as Mr. Ballou in *Roughing It*, a 60-year-old blacksmith and veteran miner who accompanied Sam Clemens and two others to Unionville.

Ward, Artemus.

Pen name of Charles Farrar Browne (born Brown), an American humorist born in Maine who began writing for the *Cleveland Plain Dealer* in 1858 and subsequently became the editor of *Vanity Fair* in New York. He traveled to Virginia City in December of 1863, becoming friends with Mark Twain, Dan De Quille, and Joseph Goodmen. Twain's story "Jim Smiley and His Jumping Frog," originally meant for one of Ward's books, was instead published in *New York Sunday Press* and picked up by other publications, becoming the catalyst to launch his career as a short-story writer and novelist. Ward went on a lecture circuit of England in 1867, during which he contracted tuberculosis and died.

Wiegand, Conrad.

Assayer in Gold Hill and publisher of the *People's Tribune* in 1870. A Philadelphia native, Wiegand was born in 1930 and came to Virginia City when he was about 33 years old, having served as assayer and coiner for the San Francisco Mint from the mid-1850s to late 1863. Wiegand feuded with Yellow Jacket Mine Superintendent John Winters, who attacked him physically, and Bank of California agent William Sharon. He later taught assaying classes in Virginia City, but his assay office there was lost in the Great Fire of 1875 His daughter and son-in-law both died young, and Wiegand hanged himself in 1880, though many, including *Enterprise* editor Joe Goodman, suspected he was a victim of foul play. Many felt that he'd been murdered, and some blamed Winters for his death.

Winters, John

Owner of a mill in Como, Winters staked a claim in Aurora around the same time Clemens was there, in 1862. Part owner of the Ophir Mine, he owned ranches in Carson City and the Washoe Valley. Despite the closure of the Como mill, Winters wasn't without a job. He was also superintendent of the Yellow Jacket Mine in Gold Hill, a position he held at the time of a catastrophic fire that claimed the lives of at least 35 miners in 1869. He ran for governor of Nevada as a Democrat in 1866, losing by just over 1,000 votes to Republican H.G. Blasdel.

Sources.

"1862 David Walley's Hot Springs Resort Celebrates 150 Years," prweb.com, June 15, 2012.

"About Lyon County Times (Silver City, Nev.) 1874-1907," Library of Congress.

"Another Pioneer Passes Away," Plumas National-Bulletin, p. 1, Oct. 1, 1914.

Antonucci, David C. "Mark Twain's Route to Lake Tahoe," Nevada Historical Society Quarterly, thomasbachand.com, June 4, 2008.

"Aurora, Nevada," forgottennevada.org.

"Aurora, Nevada," westernmininghistory.com.

"Austin and the Reese River Mining District," onlinenevada.org.

"Big Fight at Steamboat Springs," Gold Hill Daily News, p. 3, Feb. 26, 1864.

"A Bit of History," Carson City Daily Appeal, p. 2, April 16, 1921.

Brooks, Rebecca Beatrice. "Mark Twain's Civil War Experience," civilwarsaga.com, Oct. 5, 2011.

"Carson City," courthouses.co.

"Carson City Sheriff: A History," nevadaappeal.com.

"A Case of Slanderous Vilification and Its Consequences," Gold Hill Daily News, p. 3, Jan. 17, 1870.

Cegavske, Barbara K. "A Political History of Nevada," twelfth edition, leg.state.nv.us.

"Certain Death," Gold Hill Daily News, p. 2, Feb. 7, 1870.

Clapp, Nicholas. "Bodie: Good Times & Bad," sunbeltpublications.com.

"Clemens, Mary E. (Mollie) (1834-1904)," marktwainproject.org.

Clifton, Guy. "An artifact of Mark Twain's 'Duel that Never Was,'" rgj.com, Dec. 8, 2014.

"Como," ghosttowns.com.

"Como, Nevada," nvtami.com.

Daugherty, William. "Alva Gould – Discoverer of the Famous Gould and Curry Mine," legendsofamerica.com, 1891.

"David Walley's Resort," travelnevada.com. "Dayton, 1864, Lake Bigler," sites.google.com/site/bascojoenv.

"Death Calls Mark Twain's Discoverer," Sausalito News, p. 2, Oct. 6, 1917.

De Quille, Dan. "History of the Big Bonanza," American Publishing Co., University of Virginia, 1877.

De Quille, Dan. "On the Look-out for the Menken," The Golden Era, Oct. 11, 1863.

"Destructive Fire in Unionville," Carson City Daily Appeal, p. 2, Aug. 29, 1872.

DiFrancia, Chic. "The Territorial Enterprise," nevadamagazine.com, May-June 2016.

Du Fresne, Kelli. "Two hotels and one old car," nnbw.com, May 8, 2003.

Dustman, Karen. "Dutch Nick and Empire NV," clairitage.com.

Earl, Phillip. "Tom Peasley: Firefighter, patriot, tough," Reno Gazette-Journal, p. 13C, Feb. 9, 1992.

"Empire," nv-landmarks.com.

"A Fight Anticipated," Gold Hill Daily News, p. 3, April 13, 1864.

"First Presbyterian Church 150 years and counting," recordcourier.com, June 3, 2011.

"Forget What You Heard, Nevada is the True Birthplace Of Mark Twain," travelnevada.com.

Glasscock, C.B. "The Big Bonanza: The Story of the Comstock Lode," Bobbs-Merrill, 1931.

"Gould & Curry Offices," hmdb.org.

"Gravelly Ford," ghosttowns.com.

"Great Fire of 1875," carsonpedia.com.

"A Guide to the Playbills and Tickets of Piper's Opera House Collection No. 91-33," knowledgecenter.unr.edu (archived).

Gunn, Johnny. "Julia C. Bulette: Noted Nevada Prostitute," juliacbulette.com.

"Heavy Joke," Gold Hill Daily News, p. 3, Nov. 12, 1866.

"Here is the Original of Mark Twain's Tom Sawyer," San Francisco Call, p. 25, Oct. 23, 1898.

"Historic Sutro Tunnel," travelnevada.com.

"History of Lake Tahoe," tahoeinfo.com (archived).

"History of Esmeralda County," History of Nevada, Thompson and West, 1881.

"History of Steamboat," steamboatsprings.org.

Holabird, Fred N. "A Western Assayer of the Mark Twain Period," finestknown.com.

"How I Escaped Being Killed in a Duel," storyoftheweek.loa.org.

Hummel, N.A. "General History and Resources of Washoe County, Nevada," Nevada Educational Association, 1888.

"A Hyena Loose in Paulding County," Cleveland Plain Dealer, Feb. 6, 1858.

James, Ronald M. "Mark Twain in Nevada," Nevada Historical Society Quarterly, Vol. 51, No. 2, Summer 2008.

James, Ronald M. "Monk, Greeley, Ward, and Twain: The Folkloresque of a Western Legend," Western Folklore, Summer 2017.

Jarvis, Sean. "David Walley's Hot Springs Resort – Genoa, Nevada," tophotsprings.com, Dec. 30, 2022.

Joe Curtis interview, October 2022.

"John Devers 'Davies' Winters Jr.," findagrave.com.

"John Hearst of the Long Canes," amcolan.info.

"John Millian," murderpedia.org.

"A Jolly Couple," Gold Hill Daily News, p. 2, Dec. 23, 1863.

Jones, Peggy. "Mark Twain in Unionville, Nevada," literarytraveler.com, July 16, 2005.

"The Journals of Alfred Doten, 1849-1903," clark.dotendiaries.org.

"Judge Oliver, Pal of Mark Twain From Pioneer Days, Dies," Sausalito News, p. 2, March 5, 1921.

Kent, Mrs. Robert. "Ragtown – Landmark of the Past," Reno Evening Gazette, p. 2, June 21, 1958.

"The Late James W. Nye," New Orleans Republican, p. 3, Jan. 2, 1877.

Lauterborn, David. "Ghost Towns: Bodie, California," historynet.com, Sept. 20, 2018.

Lea, Ralph and Kennedy, Christi. "Reuel Gridley and a sack of flour," Lodi News-Sentinel, p. 5, Oct. 1, 2005.

Lewis, Randy. "The frog that jump-started Mark Twain's career," latimes.com, May 14, 2015.

"The Locals: The Hoaxes of Mark Twain, Dan De Quille, and Artemus Ward," alansmysteryworld.wordpress.com, July 13, 2010.

MacDonald, Douglas. "Plot to steal the capital," Reno Evening Gazette, Entertainment, p. 3, Dec. 8, 1972.

"The Mackay Mansion of Virginia City, Nevada," westernmininghistory.com.

"Mark Twain and the Empire Street Massacre of 1863," windowthroughtime.wordpress.com, Aug. 19, 2019.

"Mark Twain on Artemus Ward," New York Times, Jan. 2, 1880.

"Mark Twain part of town's history," Reno Gazette-Journal, p. 3B, April 7, 1991.

"Mark Twain's First Success," New York Times, June 25, 1899.

McGrath, Roger D. "Gunfighters, Highwaymen & Vigilantes: Violence on the Frontier," University of California Press, Berkeley, 1984.

McGrath, Roger D. "The Silver Kings," Irish America Magazine, October-November, 2012.

"Mines and Mining History," virginiacitynv.com.

Moreno, Richard. "The Nevada Traveler: Star City: Once a hub of Northern Nevada," nevadaappeal.com, Feb. 10, 2021.

Nelson, Gordon L. "Langton's Humboldt Express," Western Express, Vol. 70, No. 1, March 2020.

"Nevada Revenue – Stamped Checks, Drafts and Certificates of Deposit – 1862 to 1902," renostamp.org.

"The New County," Gold Hill Evening News, p. 2, Feb. 1, 1865.

"New historic marker to be dedicated at Spooner," nnbw.com, Nov. 29, 2001.

"News from Chicago," (James Laird killed), Gold Hill Daily News, p. 2, Jan. 16, 1869.

"The Oldest Bar In Nevada Has A Fascinating History," onliyinyourstate.com.

"On the Comstock," San Francisco Examiner, p. 36, Oct. 20, 1889.

"Once-Lively Aurora Still Has One Prospector Resident," Nevada State Journal, p. 16, Dec. 17, 1944.

Penrose, Kelsey. "Nevada Lore Series: Abe Curry and the Founding of Carson City," carsonnow.org, Jan. 17, 2019.

People's Tribune announcement, Elko Independent, p. 2, Jan. 19, 1870.

Perea, Robert. "A grand day for a grand marshal," rgj.com, Oct. 29, 2014.

"The Petrified Man," hoaxes.org.

"Piper's Opera House," travelnevada.com.

"Ragtown (Leeteville)," nvexpeditions.com.

Rasmussen, R. Kent. "Mark Twain A-Z," Oxford University Press, New York, 1995.

Reed, Jim. "Mark Twain's First Letter," Nevada Traveler, nevadagram.com, Oct. 13, 2022.

"Removal of the Capital," Gold Hill Daily News, p. 2, Feb. 15, 1864.

Robertson, T.W. and Hingston, E.P., Artemus Ward's Panorama, G.W. Carleton, London,1869.

Robison, Ken. "Samuel Clemens goes to war, bails on the whole affair," greatfallstribune.com, Nov. 29, 2014.

Rose, Mark. "When Giants Roamed the Earth, archaeology.com (archived), 2009.

Scharnhorst, Gary. "The Life of Mark Twain: The Early Years, 1835-1871," University of Missouri Press, 2018.

Schmidt, Barbara. "Chronology of Known Mark Twain Speeches, Public Readings, and Lectures," twainquotes.com.

Seitz, Don Carlos. "Artemus Ward (Charles Farrar Browne): A Biography and Bibliography," Harper & Brothers, 1919.

"The Senator and his Secretary," senate.gov.

"The Sharon Families in California," billputman.com.

Simpson, Louise. "Steamboat Hot Springs… also known as Chicken Soup Springs," montreuxreno.com, May 24, 2016.

"SLC to Mary E. (Molly) Clemens, 20 May 1864," marktwainproject.org.

Sprunger, Bud. "Ghost Town Has Population of Only One," Tacoma News Tribune, p. B1, July 12, 1959.

"St. Charles Hotel," carsonpedia.com.

Steamboat Springs item, Gold Hill Daily News, p. 3, Dec. 5, 1863.

Steamboat Springs item, Gold Hill Daily News, p. 2, June 3, 1864.

Stewart, Bob. "Forest Service wrong to deny 'Clemens Cove,'" tahoedailytribune.com, May 29, 2011.

Stewart, Robert E. "Same Clemens's Friends at Lake Tahoe," go.gale.com.

Stewart, Robert. "Mark Twain's 'Irish Brigade' from Roughing It," twainquotes.com.

"A Strange Case of Public Assault," Gold Hill Daily News, p. 3, Jan. 13, 1870.

"The Tahoe Name Game," tahoecountry.com.

Trego, Peggy. "Como Was Tops in Ambition and Horseplay During the Years It Occupied Its Hilltop," Nevada State Journal, p. 6, Feb. 21, 1954.

Twain, Mark. "Anticipating the Gridley Flour Sack History," Virginia City Territorial Enterprise, May 20, 1864.

Twain, Mark. "The Autobiography of Mark Twain," standardebooks.org.

Twain, Mark. "A Big Thing in Washoe City," Virginia City Territorial Enterprise, Dec. 23, 1862.

Twain, Mark. "Curious Changes," The Chicago Republican, May 31, 1868.

Twain, Mark. "A Ghost Story, americalliterature.com, 1870.

Twain, Mark. "Grand Austin Sanitary Flour-Sack Progress Through Storey and Lyon Counties!" Virginia City Territorial Enterprise, May 17, 1864, 1862.

Twain, Mark. "The Great Prize Fight," The Golden Era, Oct. 11, 1863.

Twain, Mark. "The Innocents Abroad," American Publishing Co., Hartford, Conn., 1869.

Twain, Mark. "Letter from Dayton," Virginia City Territorial Enterprise, February 1864.

Twain, Mark. "Letter from Mark Twain" (Steamboat Springs Hotel), Virginia City Territorial Enterprise, August 25, 1863.

Twain, Mark. "Letters from Mark Twain," Virginia City Territorial Enterprise, December 1863.

Twain, Mark. "Personal Correspondence," Virginia City Territorial Enterprise, May 24, 1864.

Twain, Mark. "The Private History of a Campaign That Failed," classicshorts.com.

Twain, Mark. "Prize fight in Washoe Valley Fourteen Rounds Fought Bloody Affray at the Close," Virginia City Territorial Enterprise, Sept. 23, 1863.

Twain, Mark. "Reese River at San Francisco," Virginia City Territorial Enterprise, July 1, 1863.

Twain, Mark. "The Removal of the Capital," Virginia City Territorial Enterprise, Feb. 16, 1864.

Twain, Mark. "Roughing It," 1872.

Twain, Mark. "A Sunday in Carson," Virginia City Territorial Enterprise, Feb. 24, 1863.

Unionville Catholic church notice, Carson City Daily Appeal, p. 2, Aug. 22, 1872.

"Unionville, Nevada," westernmininghistory.com.

"Veteran Journalist Passes Away," Reno Evening Gazette, p. 8, Nov. 12, 1903.

Weiser-Alexander, Kathy. "Henry 'Hank' Monk – Famous Stage Driver of the Old West," legendsofamerica.com, May 2020.

"Wholesome Arrest," Sacramento Daily Union, p. 2, July 30, 1863.

Also by the author

Historical nonfiction

Yesterday's Highways
America's Loneliest Road
The Lincoln Highway in California (with Gary Kinst)
America's First Highways
Highways of the South
The Great American Shopping Experience
Martinsville Memories
Fresno Growing Up
Fresno Century
Goldfield Century
Carson City Century
San Luis Obispo Century
Charleston Century
Cambria Century
Roanoke Century
Huntington Century
Danville Century
Greensboro Century
Highway 99: The History of California's Main Street
Highway 101: The History of El Camino Real
The Legend of Molly Bolin
A Whole Different League

Fiction

The Talismans of Time
Pathfinder of Destiny
Nightmare's Eve
Death's Doorstep
Memortality
Paralucidity
The Only Dragon
Identity Break
Feathercap

Praise for other works

"If you have any interest in highways, old diners and motels and such, or 20th century US history, this book is for you. It is without a doubt one of the best highway books ever published."

— Dan R. Young, founder OLD HIGHWAY 101 group, on
Yesterday's Highways

"Profusely illustrated throughout, **Highway 99** is unreservedly recommended as an essential and core addition to every community and academic library's California History collections."

— California Bookwatch

"... an engaging narrative that pulls the reader into the story and onto the road. ... I highly recommend **Highway 99: The History of California's Main Street**, whether you're a roadside archaeology nut or just someone who enjoys a ripping story peppered with vintage photographs."

— Barbara Gossett,
Society for Commercial Archaeology Journal

"The genres in this volume span horror, fantasy, and science-fiction, and each is handled deftly. ... **Nightmare's Eve** should be on your reading list. The stories are at the intersection of nightmare and lucid dreaming, up ahead a signpost ... next stop, your reading pile. Keep the nightlight on."

— R.B. Payne, Cemetery Dance

"As informed and informative as it is entertaining and absorbing, **Fresno Growing Up** is very highly recommended for personal, community, and academic library 20th Century American History collections."

— John Burroughs, Reviewer's Bookwatch

"An essential primer for anyone seeking an entrée into the genre. Provost serves up a smorgasbord of highlights gleaned from his personal memories of and research into the various nooks and crannies of what 'used-to-be' in professional team sports."

— Tim Hanlon, Good Seats Still Available, on **A Whole Different League**

"The complex idea of mixing morality and mortality is a fresh twist on the human condition. ... **Memortality** is one of those books that will incite more questions than it answers. And for fandom, that's a good thing."

— Ricky L. Brown, Amazing Stories

"Punchy and fast paced, **Memortality** reads like a graphic novel. ... (Provost's) style makes the trippy landscapes and mind-bending plot points more believable and adds a thrilling edge to this vivid crossover fantasy."

— Foreword Reviews

"**Memortality** by Stephen Provost is a highly original, thrilling novel unlike anything else out there."

— David McAfee, bestselling author of 33 A.D., 61 A.D., and 79 A.D.

"Provost sticks mostly to the classics: vampires, ghosts, aliens, and even dragons. But trekking familiar terrain allows the author to subvert readers' expectations. ... Provost's poetry skillfully displays the same somber themes as the stories. ... Worthy tales that prove external forces are no more terrifying than what's inside people's heads."

— Kirkus Reviews on **Nightmare's Eve**

About the author

Stephen H. Provost is the author of several books on 20th century America, covering topics that range from his hometown to department stores and shopping centers; from pop music and sports icons to the history of our nation's highways. During a 30-year career in journalism, he worked as a managing editor, sports editor, copy desk chief, columnist and reporter at five newspapers. As a novelist, he has written about dragons, mutant superheroes, and things that go bump in the night. A California native, he now lives in Nevada.

Did you enjoy this book?

Recommend it to a friend. And please consider rating it and/or leaving a brief review online at Amazon, Barnes & Noble and Goodreads.

Made in the USA
Middletown, DE
06 April 2023